Solving the Murder of
VIENG PHOVIXAY

Solving the Murder of

VIENG PHOVIXAY

EVIL DWELLS IN WEST GEORGIA

CLAY BRYANT

THE
History
PRESS

Published by The History Press
Charleston, SC
www.historypress.com

First published 2024

Manufactured in the United States

ISBN 9781467158596

Library of Congress Control Number: 2024938208

CONTENTS

ACKNOWLEDGEMENTS

Thank you to the following:

Gary Rothwell, for without his commitment to justice Vieng Phovixay would have never received the justice she deserved.

Pete Skandalakis, for affording me the opportunity to achieve the most rewarding accomplishments of my professional career.

Ray Mayer, for guiding me to success in finding some long overdue justice.

Dr. John Williams, without whom none of my books would have ever seen the light of day.

Sheriff Mike Jolley, who always welcomed and assisted us in every way.

Phyllis Williams, for her tireless work with the victims.

That small voice that inspires me to carry on.

PREFACE

The epic journey of the Phovixay family began as the war in Vietnam was coming to a close. In late 1972 and early 1973, as American troops were being withdrawn, Savang Phovixay and his family resided in a village in Laos just across the border from the demilitarized zone that separated North and South Vietnam.

Savang had served United States military intelligence as an interpreter and intelligence asset. As the United States withdrew and the South Vietnamese government capitulated, the North Vietnamese Army began to round up and imprison everyone they could identify who had assisted the South in the war. The North Vietnamese Army crossed the Laotian border and kidnapped Savang. He was taken across the border into North Vietnam, where he was imprisoned in a prison pit.

It would be only through the heroic actions of his wife, Khan, that Savang Phovixay would survive. His rescue would begin a journey for the Phovixays and their children that, with the help of the CIA and the U.S. State Department, would span years and thousands of miles and end in Newnan, Georgia. It would be here that Savang would find the safety for his family he had so desperately sought. Or so it would seem. Instead, it would be here that the journey of Vieng, Savang's cherished daughter, would end in unthinkable horror in a remote pine forest at the hands of a vicious predator.

How tragically ironic that the family's journey, after their epic escape from the evils that existed halfway around the world and their arrival at what they perceived as the safe haven they had sought to find in America, would end in one of their precious numbers being stolen away by the evil that dwells among us.

Chapter 1

AN EPIC JOURNEY

After the American forces withdrew from Vietnam in the spring of 1973, anyone identified as a collaborator with the Americans or the South Vietnamese government was rounded up by the North Vietnamese Army, or the Viet Cong, and summarily marked for execution. Savang Phovixay was one of their number. Savang lived just across the border in Laos with his family. Savang had served as an interpreter for American intelligence during the Vietnam Conflict.

He was kidnapped by Viet Cong forces, a guerrilla extension of the North Vietnamese Army, and taken just across the border into North Vietnam. There he was imprisoned with approximately twenty others in a prison pit, a rectangular pit approximately thirty feet long, fifteen feet wide and twelve feet deep. The pit had sheer sides that were impossible to climb. Anyone who attempted escape would be summarily executed by the lone guard posted at the pit. The pit itself was a form of execution; no one who was imprisoned therein was supposed to survive. It was not only a method of confinement but also a constant public reminder that anyone who chose to defy the authority of the North Vietnamese government would meet with the same fate.

Savang, unlike the others, had a saving grace—his wife, Khan. Khan, just like everyone in the area, was informed where her husband was and what his eventual fate would be. Khan knew she had to try something to free her husband. She was able to gather some money from members of her family and made the dangerous trek across the North Vietnamese border to where Savang was being held, and there, she was able to bribe the guard tasked with watching over the pit. Savang was pulled up on a rope, and he and Khan escaped into the jungle and back into Laos.

Knowing that he was still a marked man, Savang knew he had to take his family to a place of safety out of reach of the Viet Cong. He made a raft, and he, his wife and their two eldest daughters made their way down the Mekong River into Thailand, where they found refuge in a refugee camp. The family would stay there for the next five years. While they were there, another daughter and two sons were born, one of whom succumbed to dysentery in the refugee camp as an infant.

Savang applied for asylum to the United States. In 1979, the CIA and the State Department identified him as having been an American asset, and he and the family were granted asylum.

The Phovixay family boarded a plane in Bangkok, Thailand, and arrived in Atlanta by way of San Francisco. The First Baptist Church of Newnan, Georgia, sponsored the Phovixay family. Savang was given a job doing custodial work by the church, and the family settled in their new home. The children thrived; they quickly learned the English language, enrolled in school and did exceedingly well academically.

To Savang, the evil that had almost taken his life years before and half the world away was but a fading memory; little did he know that even in the safety of his new home, his precious family would fall victim to the evil that dwells among us.

Chapter 2

TRAGIC RESULTS
OF SYSTEM FAILURE

The purpose of the justice system is twofold: first and foremost, to protect innocent members of society from harm by those who would choose to perpetrate it; and second, to hold those individuals who commit crimes accountable to the rule of law.

The American justice system is complex, with many layers; it is recognized by many as the best in the world. When it works correctly, it is a model of fairness and equity, but when the system fails, the results are often devastatingly tragic.

In my opinion, the greatest tragedy of our system's failure is the conviction of an innocent person for a crime he or she did not commit. I would rather see one hundred crimes go unsolved than bring forth a charge that results in the wrongful conviction of one innocent man or woman.

Our justice system is a three-tiered system composed of law enforcement; the judiciary, or courts; and finally, the corrections system. All work independently and in concert with one another to ensure that justice is served and that the public is protected.

In years of dealing with Charles Travis Manley, our system failed to one degree or another at every level. I feel that some of those failures were the result of honest mistakes, some were the result of incompetence, some were beyond the control of those involved and early on in his criminal career I feel that something more nefarious could well have been involved. This allowed Manley to advance his deviant and criminal activity far beyond what should have been curtailed early on in his long list of violent crimes that dated back to the early 1970s.

History tells us that sex offenders generally begin their lives of deviant behavior with relatively lower-level offenses such as voyeurism and unwanted touchings. Left unchecked, these offenders progressively elevate their crimes to serious criminal activity that can eventually rise to physical assaults, rape, sodomy and up to and including murder. Such was the case of Charles Travis Manley.

The justice system's failure to effectively deal with Charles Manley would have devastating effects on his victims, but none greater than on Vieng Phovixay and her family. It would be these failures that would allow the progression and devastation to continue, all inflicted by the evil that was allowed to dwell among us.

Chapter 3

A TROUBLED PAST

Sometimes the development of evil in a person can't be understood or explained. In my experience, people who are raised in decent surroundings by right-minded parents seem to do well in general; they develop good morals and function well in society. I have seen people who come from broken homes and horrible life situations grow up, and they, too, overcome and do well. Then there are those few who come from good homes and supportive families but for whatever reason just become sociopaths consumed by and controlled by an evil from within. Charles Travis Manley was one of those people.

Charles was born to an average working-class family in West Point, Georgia, on November 11, 1946. Ironically, I knew his father long before I ever heard the name Charles Manley. In 1976, as a rookie Georgia state trooper, I met Lieutenant A.C. Manley of the West Point Police Department. I regarded Lieutenant Manley as a good man, always exhibiting a respectful and kind demeanor. Knowing what I know now, I find it hard to believe that Charles Travis Manley could have been raised by the A.C. Manley that I knew.

By all accounts from family members and people who knew Charles, he was a somewhat troubled youth. Charles was the only child of A.C. and Iodie Manley. His father and mother divorced, and he was raised by his mother in Heard County, Georgia. He attended and graduated from Heard County High School. He struggled in school both academically and socially.

He often experienced discipline issues in school. After he graduated from high school, he moved back to West Point and married his first wife.

He worked wherever he could find a job. He began to work in garages as a mechanic and later acquired the skills to become a truck driver. In his younger years, he spent most of his free time hanging out just across the state line in a pool hall in Lanett, Alabama. Family members stated that he developed a drinking problem at a relatively early age.

It would be his relationship with women that was most troubling. Charles Manley was married four times; he had five children, all with his first wife—three daughters and two sons. The marriage lasted ten years and ended in divorce while he was serving a prison sentence for a 1973 rape conviction. He would be married three subsequent times, two of which ended in divorce.

When trying to find the dark secrets of a man, one needs to look no further than his ex-girlfriends and ex-wives. In this case, I researched all previous wives and women involved with Charles Manley I could find. They proved to be a storehouse of knowledge and insight into the mind and sociopathic tendencies of Charles Travis Manley. They would provide information that would lead us to other crimes and other victims.

The past women in his life described his personality as somewhat like that of a Dr. Jekyll and Mr. Hyde. He could be subdued and rational one minute and hostile and violent the next. According to his ex-wives, his relationship with women was most troubling; he was violent and displayed sexually deviant tendencies toward the ones with whom I spoke. They related that this was exhibited most when he was under the influence of alcohol or drugs.

Manley was described as being sexually sadistic. His ex-wives described instances of violent marital rape and sodomy. One of the wives agreed to testify and did so at trial as a similar circumstance witness for the prosecution. She told of an incident in her interview in which Manley came home from drinking and they got into an argument, during which he struck her several times in the face. She went on to say that while she was in the bathroom washing the blood off her face, Charles grabbed her from behind, held a kitchen knife to her throat and told her he'd kill her if she fought him. He then proceeded to anally rape her.

She stated that she was afraid of him to this day. She said that she was of the opinion that Manley was well capable of murder during a rape, especially if he was drinking. It would be the allowing of this process of progression to continue that would lead to the tragic events of the fall of 1987.

Charles Manley displayed the conduct and actions of a true sociopath. He could be disarming in his demeanor and actions. But when something triggered the demon within him, he became an absolute monster. His actions seemed to be totally outrageous and beyond his control. For whatever reason, when that switch was flipped, terrible things were about to happen.

It would be Manley's history of avoiding equitable justice that would be responsible for his long list of devastated victims. He was truly an evil that was allowed to dwell among us.

Chapter 4

1971: THE ONSET OF EVIL

O n a late fall evening in 1971, a teenage couple identified as Roger Garner and Betty Moore sat just off the road that led to Chambers Academy in Chambers County, Alabama. This was an area known as a lovers' lane for young couples. As they sat in the car, they were approached by an individual who asked them for a light for his cigarette. Roger Garner recognized the man from seeing him on occasion in the pool room in Lanett as Charles Manley. The young man gave Manley a light, and he walked away.

Manley again approached the car without being detected. As the couple sat and talked, the girl sat with her back against the driver's door, and the young man was in the front passenger seat. Without warning, the driver's door was snatched open and the young woman was grabbed in a chokehold by Manley, who held a knife to her throat.

While holding the knife to her throat, Manley ordered the young man to get into the trunk of the vehicle. There was no mistaking Manley's intentions, as he threatened to kill her unless they complied with his demands. The young woman, however, struggled with Manley, during which she received defensive wounds to her hand but managed to knee her assailant in the groin. This loosened his grip, and she was able to get free and get to the other side of the car before Manley could recover. After a brief pursuit around the car, the heavyset Manley realized he could not catch Moore, who was able to keep the car between them. An exhausted

Manley tried to apologize for what he had done. He warned the couple not to notify the police. He then fled the scene.

The couple immediately reported the event to the police. Charles Travis Manley was arrested and initially charged with one count of aggravated assault with intent to rape and one count of aggravated assault on the male victim, both serious felonies with possible lengthy prison sentences. Manley was held in the Chambers County jail awaiting trial on what appeared to be a solid case against him.

On March 29, 1972, Charles Travis Manley was brought into the Circuit Court of Chambers County, Alabama, before Judge W.C. Hines, where inexplicably and outside the presence of the victims he was allowed to enter into a plea agreement. He was allowed to plead guilty to a single misdemeanor count of assault and battery. Manley was fined $125 and released to time served. Considering the magnitude of violence involved in the case, it is unfathomable that such a light sentence was imposed. I find it hard to believe, with the facts as they were, that Manley would receive a slap on the wrist and be set free.

It would be only a short time before this and subsequent failures to recognize and deal with Charles Manley for the danger that he posed to society would allow this intensifying evil to dwell among us.

Chapter 5

1973: THE PROGRESSION OF EVIL

Charles Manley must have certainly been emboldened by the result of his previous prosecution in Chambers County. Had Betty Moore not been able to escape Manley's grasp, that situation very probably would not have ended well for his victims.

After being allowed to walk out of the courtroom after facing those charges, he had to feel ten feet tall and bulletproof. It would be only a short while before the evil that was allowed to dwell among us would once again raise its ugly head.

Charles Manley's father, A.C. Manley, lived alone and had a woman who cleaned and kept house for him. She was familiar with A.C.'s son, Charles; however, she knew nothing about his previous criminal incident a mere year earlier.

On October 10, 1973, at approximately 7:30 p.m., Charles called the woman and said he needed a babysitter. In the past, the woman's fifteen-year-old daughter had babysat for Manley and his wife. A short time later, Manley arrived at the home of the woman just across the state line in Lanett, Alabama, to pick up the young girl. The mother had usually dealt with Manley's wife, and on such short notice she told Manley that she was going to send her fifteen-year-old and her twelve-year-old. Manley agreed to take both girls.

Instead of taking the girls to his home, Manley drove north of West Point, Georgia, on U.S. 29 and onto a county dirt road and then a remote logging road. After stopping the car, Manley produced a .44-caliber pistol and forced the twelve-year-old out of the car at gunpoint. He then proceeded to rape the older sister at gunpoint. At some point, Manley realized the younger child had run away, and while he was searching for her, the older girl was able to escape and hide in the woods. Being unable to locate either of the girls, Manley got into his car and drove off. After Manley left, the girls reunited, walked to a residence and called their father, who came and got them.

When the girls related to their parents what had happened, they immediately called the police. Troup County chief deputy Jerry Bryan interviewed the girls, both of whom positively identified Charles Manley as the person responsible for the crime.

Bryan obtained a warrant for Manley's arrest, charging him with one count of rape. During an interview with Deputy Bryan, Manley confessed to the crime. He was held in the Troup County jail and brought before Judge Lamar Knight on November 15, 1973. He was allowed to enter a plea of guilty to the offense of rape and given a nine-year sentence for raping a young Black girl at gunpoint. For a crime that could carry up to a life sentence, Manley was for some reason given a sentence that was unexplainably light, considering the circumstances.

To add insult to injury, Manley was released on parole in 1979 after serving fewer than six years of his nine-year sentence.

Free once again, Charles Travis Manley would quickly assume his role as the evil that dwells among us.

Chapter 6

1980: THE CONTINUATION OF EVIL

Having been released to parole in 1979 after serving only six years of a nine-year prison sentence for the at-gunpoint rape of a young girl, Charles Manley was once again a free man.

While he was in prison, his first wife filed for and obtained a divorce from Manley. Upon his release, he quickly married Linda Boettcher. Less than a year after his early release from prison, Manley was charged with the February 19, 1980 burglary of the residence of Emma Sue Searcy on Webb Road in rural Troup County, Georgia. An eyewitness identified Manley and described his clothing and vehicle used during the burglary.

A search warrant was obtained for his residence at 405 Cherry Valley Drive in Lanett, Alabama. At the residence, officers found the vehicle described by the witness, along with items taken from the residence, including a high standard revolver, currency and clothing matching the description given by the witness.

Manley was arrested and charged with the burglary. This time, he refused to give a statement to the police. At his preliminary hearing, Manley pleaded not guilty. Charles Travis Manley was indicted in May 1980 by the Troup County Grand Jury for the burglary of the Searcy residence. The case went to trial before a jury on May 21, 1980, once again before Judge Lamar Knight. On May 22, 1980, the jury found Manley guilty of the crime.

I find it puzzling that Judge Knight gave Manley a sentence of sixteen years for a burglary that involved less than $300 worth of property after having issued him only a nine-year sentence for a violent kidnapping and rape at gunpoint.

Manley appealed the sentence before the Georgia Sentence Review Panel. At that time, any sentence over five years not eligible for the death penalty was eligible for sentence administrative review upon appeal. Upon review of the case and conviction, the Sentence Review Panel upheld the trial court's sentence of sixteen years to serve in the state prison system.

In reviewing Manley's Department of Corrections file, I discovered that he had been a less than stellar prisoner. He was administratively disciplined for smuggling alcohol into the prison. He had obtained trustee status and was allowed to drive a prison vehicle in his role as a mechanic. He was caught bringing beer and wine into the facility. According to his classification file and his ongoing psychological examination prior to his parole determination, Manley demonstrated several psychological tendencies consistent with the profile of a sociopath. The report stated that he was found to be manipulative; held contempt for authority; saw himself as mentally superior to others, especially women; displayed violent behavior; and showed no remorse for his crimes.

Yet considering all this, he was inexplicably granted early release to parole on September 1, 1985. It would be this regrettable and tragic decision that would lead to a horrible discovery in a remote forest in Harris County, Georgia, in 1987 and other unspeakable acts to follow, all committed by the evil that was allowed to dwell among us.

Chapter 7

OCTOBER 10, 1987: VANISHED

Vieng Phovixay had just graduated from Newnan High School as an honor student, a remarkable achievement considering the obstacles that she and her family had faced. She had been offered an academic scholarship. She was deeply involved in her church. It was during her senior year that she met a young man named Kenneth Baker and began a romantic relationship with him. He had moved in with Vieng and her family, and later the couple moved into a trailer of their own for a short while. She had gotten a job at Thriftway grocery in Newnan after her high school graduation.

That fall, her relationship with Baker became troubled. Baker moved in with a friend at lot 7 of the Moreland Trailer Park. On the morning of October 10, 1987, Vieng got ready to go to work and left the home where she and her siblings lived with their parents at 8 Hollis Heights in Newnan. She was to work at Thriftway grocery store that afternoon. She traveled to Moreland, Georgia, which is located just south of Newnan in Coweta County, with the intent of visiting Baker in the Moreland Trailer Park.

Investigators later discovered that Vieng stopped at the convenience store located on U.S. Highway 29 just north of Moreland sometime around 10:00 a.m. She entered the store, purchased some items, returned to her car and drove away. A short time later, Vieng telephoned her home and said she had a flat tire on U.S. 29 as she was leaving the convenience store. Her father, Savang, was contacted at work, and he said that he would leave work and come to Vieng's rescue.

Vieng Phovixay. *Courtesy of the Phovixay family.*

Shortly thereafter, Vieng arrived at the residence of Kenneth Baker at the Moreland Trailer Park. According to Baker and other witnesses, she arrived in a 1975 Chevrolet El Camino that was blueish green with a white vinyl top. It displayed the iconic SS package of emblems and striping and also had American Mag wheels and a Rebel flag license plate on the front of the vehicle. All descriptions given were very explicit and consistent.

Vieng told Baker of the flat tire and that the man driving the El Camino had stopped to help her and offered to take her to Baker's house. Baker and two independent witnesses spoke with the man, described as approximately six feet tall, heavyset, with a full beard and a beer belly and wearing dark shaded glasses.

It was from Baker's residence that Vieng called her home to report her dilemma. After speaking to Baker and two witnesses, neighbors Johnny and Darlene Wentz, the man got into the car and left.

According to Baker, sometime later the unknown man in the El Camino returned and stated that he had obtained a tire from a friend who lived nearby and that he would take Vieng back to the car with the tire so she could be on her way. At that point, she got into the El Camino with the man and left. That was the last time anyone reported seeing Vieng Phovixay.

Vieng's father, Savang, arrived at her car on the roadside, but Vieng was nowhere to be found. After a fruitless search for his daughter, Savang returned home. As afternoon turned into nightfall, there was still no sign of Vieng. She did not show up to work at the Thriftway grocery, which was totally out of character for her. Saturday night came and went with no sign of Vieng.

The family was frantic as they contacted friends and church members in the hope someone would shed some light on Vieng's whereabouts. After finding no one who had had contact with Vieng, they contacted the Newnan police and reported her missing. It was quickly determined that Vieng had last been seen in Moreland, in unincorporated Coweta County, and the case was handed to the Coweta County Sheriff's Office.

On October 13, a statewide missing person's broadcast was put out to law enforcement relating to the disappearance of Vieng Phovixay and the surrounding circumstances. The broadcast yielded no immediate results, and on the following day, October 14, with mounting public concern and the possibility of suspected foul play, the sheriff's office requested investigative assistance from the Georgia Bureau of Investigation. Agent A.H. Davis was assigned to the case. Davis met with sheriff's investigators Donnie Payne and Mike Yeager, who filled him in on what had transpired in the case so far.

Agent Davis was told Phovixay had been missing since Saturday and was told of the events that had been reported. The investigation into Vieng's disappearance had begun in earnest. Had she simply decided to walk away, or had she fallen prey to an unknown evil that dwelled among us?

Chapter 8

PIECES OF THE PUZZLE

Missing person cases can be an investigative nightmare. There is always an aura of mystery surrounding a missing person case, and this leads to suspicion, opinions and conjecture. It can be those things that can lead to the truth of what has happened, or they can take the case down a rabbit hole that is all but impossible to dig out of.

In 1987 in Newnan, Georgia, the news of Vieng's disappearance traveled like wildfire through the community; even before the case was officially opened, because of her church affiliation and ties to the community, her disappearance was widespread knowledge. Many church members, teachers and friends were quickly made aware of the situation. And quite a few of these, because of their relationship with Vieng and their knowledge of what was going on in her life, had strong opinions as to what might have happened to her.

Within a couple of days, her going missing was general knowledge in the community, and there was no shortage of discussion of the circumstances surrounding her disappearance. People began to come forward with information even before the investigators got started on the case.

The investigators began the investigation in earnest as soon as it was handed to them. The logical place to start, of course, was where Vieng was last seen. It would be there that the investigators would start to gather their facts and information.

On October 14, a preliminary canvass of the trailer park was conducted, and it revealed several items that seemed to be pertinent information. Judy

Collins, one of the residents, informed investigators that she had seen an El Camino, which she described as being green and sporty looking, with mag wheels, parked in front of lot 7, which was the trailer where Kenneth Baker was staying. After going to the store and returning at about 2:15 p.m., Collins told investigators she had seen a lone person in the car, and he was driving away.

As word got out that Vieng had disappeared from the Moreland area, investigator Mike Yeager was contacted on the afternoon of October 14 by Carl Pratt, who stated that around noon on Saturday, he had been driving on U.S. 29 and on the side of the road across from Gas Incorporated he saw an "Oriental girl" standing beside a car that appeared to have a flat tire.

Meanwhile, Agent Davis was interviewing Johnny and Darlene Wentz at their residence at lot 6, which was directly across from lot 7. Johnny Wentz stated that he and his wife were outside when they saw Vieng Phovixay ride up to Baker's residence at lot 7 in a greenish-blue Chevrolet El Camino driven by a white male whom he described as heavyset, with a beard and dark glasses. Wentz went on to say he approached the man and asked about the car. They spoke about the car; Wentz stated that he was interested in the vehicle, as he had owned an El Camino in the past. He said he believed the car was a 1975 SS with white stripes and mag wheels. Wentz said he thought he recognized the man as someone he had seen hanging out at P.J.'s Lounge and Southside 29 Lounge, both located in Newnan.

Darlene Wentz said that around eleven o'clock on Saturday she saw a dark-colored El Camino drive into the trailer park driven by a heavyset guy with a full beard. She described the car as having white stripes and white letter tires. She went on to say that Vieng Phovixay got out of the front passenger seat. Wentz stated that she knew Phovixay personally and had talked with her on many occasions. She was familiar with the fact that she was in a relationship with Kenneth Baker. Wentz went on to say Vieng asked if she knew if Baker was home. Wentz said Vieng said she had a flat tire, and the man she was with had stopped to help her and agreed to bring her to the trailer park.

She said that at that point, Vieng went to the door at lot 7 and knocked. The door was answered by Ken Baker, who came out and spoke with Vieng and the man in the El Camino. She went on to say that then Baker and Phovixay went inside the residence at lot 7, and the man in the El Camino drove out of the trailer park.

Wentz further stated that after a while, the El Camino returned, and the driver engaged in a conversation with Phovixay and Baker, after which

Phovixay got in the El Camino with the man and left. That was the last time she ever saw Vieng Phovixay, the El Camino or the man who was driving it.

Up to this point, the one consistent piece of information garnered from all the witnesses was that the last time Vieng Phovixay was seen, she was leaving the trailer park with a man in the very distinctive El Camino. Over the next few days, investigators continued to conduct interviews and search for information regarding Vieng's disappearance.

Hours and days passed without any word or contact from Vieng. From all indications, the possibility that she would voluntarily disappear without any word to her family or close friends was totally out of character and inconceivable to all who knew her.

The realization had set in that quite possibly Vieng had fallen prey to a terrible evil that dwells among us.

Chapter 9

A SHIFT IN FOCUS

ven though a few days passed, during which there was no new information in the case, the one fact that seemed substantial was the man in the El Camino, whom independent witnesses all gave consistent descriptions of and remembered last seeing Vieng driving away with. The investigators began to turn to friends and associates, anyone whom Vieng may have confided in who could possibly shed some light on the circumstances surrounding her disappearance.

On Thursday, October 15, five days after Vieng's disappearance, Agent Davis interviewed Tanya Quick. Quick told Davis that she felt she was Vieng's best friend and had been for several years. Quick said that Vieng and Baker had broken up a couple months prior and she had moved back in with her parents in Hollis Heights. She said that on several occasions, Vieng had come to her house crying after Baker had struck her. Quick stated that Baker was quick tempered and controlling, even to the point of him telling Quick to stay away from Vieng.

Quick went on to say that about a month or so earlier, Vieng had come to her and said that she was pregnant. Quick said Vieng was confused and apprehensive about having the baby, but later Vieng said she was having the baby and was enthusiastic about it. Quick said Vieng told her that she had told Baker about the baby and that he had gotten angry and demanded she have an abortion. According to Quick, Vieng refused the idea and told Baker that she was going to tell his grandparents about the baby. Baker told Vieng that if she did, he'd kill her.

Quick ended by saying that in her opinion Vieng was an intelligent and responsible person. She said it was totally uncharacteristic of her not to have contacted someone to let them know where she was and that she was all right.

The information obtained from Quick raised a red flag with investigators, who began to question whether Baker could have had a motive to make Vieng disappear.

Hoping to find some more insight into things that were going on in Vieng's life, Davis turned next to Don Helms, an associate pastor at the First Baptist Church of Newnan. Helms stated that his church had sponsored the Phovixay family upon their seeking asylum in the United States. He said that church members had done all things possible to get the family settled into their new home, including teaching them English and helping them acclimate into American culture. He described Vieng as intelligent, quiet and artistic.

He went on to say that about six months earlier, he had noticed Ken Baker spending a lot of time at Vieng's parents' house at 8 Hollis Heights. Helms said that around that time, he noticed changes in Vieng's personality. Helms expressed deep concern for Vieng's safety, noting that he believed she would have reached out to her family or a church member by now unless something dreadful had happened to her.

Later that day, Agent Davis went to Collins Middle School and spoke with Nancy Stoltz, a teacher at the school and friend of the Phovixay family. Stoltz stated that she had met Vieng Phovixay when her church sponsored the family to come to the United States. She had helped teach them English and helped them adapt to life in America. She was very close to Vieng and served as a mentor to her.

Stoltz stated that in April 1987, Vieng told her she was going to marry Ken Baker. At about that time, Stoltz said she noticed a change in Vieng's personality, that she was not as outgoing and open as she had been. She went on to say that on Friday, October 2, 1987, Vieng came to see her and talked to her about her relationship with Baker. Vieng told her they had broken up. Then on October 9, Vieng called and was upset; she told Stolz that she was pregnant and did not know what she was going to do. Stoltz said she consoled Vieng and told her to think of the positives of having a baby. By the end of their conversation, Stoltz said that Vieng said she would keep the baby and was looking forward to doing so.

Stoltz closed by saying that Vieng was not the type of individual who would run away and not let someone know her whereabouts.

While at the Collins Middle School, Agent Davis also spoke with Amphay Phovixay, Vieng's fourteen-year-old sister. Amphay told Davis that it was she who had answered the phone when Vieng called to say she had a flat tire and needed her father's help. Amphay said that for the past few months, Vieng had become sullen and moody, especially when Ken Baker was present. The sister said that Vieng had told her on several occasions that she feared Baker and that he had hit and beat her on occasion in the last few months.

Amphay told Davis that when Vieng called about the tire around eleven o'clock that morning asking for her father's help, she seemed to be upset and maybe crying. Amphay contacted her father at work. She said Savang came home at about noon and then left to go assist Vieng. She said that was the last time she ever heard from her sister.

Later that day, Davis went to the residence of Savang Phovixay at 8 Hollis Heights in Newnan. In his interview, Savang stated that Vieng had left the house at about 7:00 a.m. and he had gone to work at Kroger. When he arrived home at about noon, he was told about Vieng's flat tire and that she needed his help.

He left home and arrived at her car in front of Gas Inc. on U.S. 29 just north of Moreland. The car had a flat tire, and he put the spare on the car. The tire had what appeared to be a cut in the sidewall.

Vieng was nowhere to be found. Savang left a note on her car for her to see and then went home. When Vieng had not returned home or called by 6:00 p.m., he again went to where the car was located; the note was still on the windshield. He then drove the car home. Savang stated that Vieng and Ken had lived with them for about a month and that Ken constantly spoke harshly and intimidated Vieng.

As time passed, it was becoming increasingly apparent to everyone involved that this was not going to end well and that Vieng had fallen victim to an evil that dwelled among us.

Chapter 10

DOWN THE RABBIT HOLE

A s the case progressed, it became obvious that Vieng's family and friends all had developed the opinion that if anything nefarious had happened to Vieng, her boyfriend, Ken Baker, was the number one suspect.

The opinion of those concerned and familiar with Vieng's situation, in my opinion, unduly influenced the direction of the investigation. When investigators gained knowledge of Vieng's domestic situation, the investigative spotlight began to shine brightly on Kenneth Baker.

It is absolutely essential to have an open mind to every possibility when you are dealing with the unknown of a missing person's case. It is, however, also important not to forget the cardinal rule of a missing person or homicide investigation: start with the known and begin the elimination process from there unless an epiphany arises that demands a change in course. Start with what you know.

Sheriff Larry Hammett interviewed Kenneth Baker on November 11, 1987. Baker was advised of his Miranda rights and waived his right to have an attorney present. Early in the interview, Baker was asked what he could tell them about Vieng's disappearance. Baker stated that Vieng had come to his house that Saturday morning at about eight or nine o'clock. He stated he was still in bed, and Vieng came in and sat on the bed and began talking about the pregnancy.

Baker said he told her he would pay for an abortion, or if she kept the baby, he'd pay child support. According to Baker, she stayed with him for an hour or so, and they talked about getting back together. He went on to say he told her he needed time to think about it; at that point, she became upset and told him he could not visit the child unless he came back to her. Baker said Vieng then went to her car and took a nerve pill and left.

According to Baker, a short time later he heard a car pull up outside. When he looked out, he saw Vieng getting out of a Chevrolet El Camino driven by a white male. He opened the door and found Vieng sitting on the steps. Baker said he asked Vieng who the man was she was with, and she told him she'd had a flat tire and the man had stopped to help her and she asked him to take her to Baker's.

Baker went on to say that Vieng went to the pay phone to call her father. Vieng returned to Baker's and came inside. A short time later, the man in the El Camino came back to the door and asked if the girl he had brought there was still there. Baker said the man said he had gotten a tire and would take her back and fix her tire if she would like for him to help. Baker stated he asked her if she wanted to go with the man, and she said yes. She then got in the El Camino and they left, and that was the last time he had seen or heard from Vieng.

When asked if he and Vieng ever fought, Baker replied their fights were only verbal; he did say they argued often but that he never hit her. When asked whether he and Vieng were married, he said they never formally married but he had been told because they had lived together they were common-law husband and wife. Baker was asked if he had ever seen the El Camino before, and he said that he had not. When asked if he had any idea where Vieng might be, he said he did not.

Baker was asked if he would submit to a polygraph test regarding the disappearance of Vieng Phovixay. He stated that he would do so voluntarily.

Later that day, on November 11, Baker was interviewed and administered a polygraph examination by Georgia Bureau of Investigation agent Tom Davis. According to Agent Davis, Baker passed the polygraph with no problem. All the pertinent questions regarding the disappearance of Phovixay revealed no deception.

Due to the circumstances that surrounded her disappearance and her tenuous relationship with Baker, in the case of the disappearance of Vieng Phovixay, Kenneth Baker was as good as convicted in the court of public opinion.

With no news or progress on the case, in mid-November, the investigators turned to the news media for help. While the Newnan local media was following the case and giving it a lot of local exposure, investigators turned to the Atlanta television market for assistance.

The story of Vieng's disappearance was aired on all three network affiliates in Atlanta. The piece contained information on the last time Vieng was seen. There was a detailed description of the El Camino and its driver. It was a long shot, but the hope was that the publicity might create information that would breathe new life into the case and shine new light on the evil that dwelled among us.

Chapter 11

EPIPHANY LOST

It has been said it's always darkest before the dawn. This old maxim holds a lot of truth when it comes to criminal investigations. Sometimes you arrive at an impasse, progress ceases and no new evidence or information comes forth to propel the case into the light. And then, just when the case seems stuck, a glimmer of light comes. If you are lucky enough to have such an epiphany, you can't close your eyes and remain in darkness. You must turn toward the light.

The television exposure of the case caught the eye of state parole officer Mike Spear. Seeing the newscast about the disappearance of Vieng Phovixay, Spear realized he had information that could possibly lead to a viable suspect and a break in the case.

Spear contacted the Coweta County Sheriff's Office in mid-November with information that he had a parolee who closely fit the description given in the disappearance of Vieng Phovixay. Spear also informed the investigators that the parolee, Charles Manley, drove a Chevrolet El Camino that was very similar to the description of the vehicle on the television broadcast.

Spear went on to inform the police that Manley had been convicted of a kidnapping and rape of a young girl in 1973 and received a nine-year prison sentence for that crime, and currently he was on parole for burglary, for which he had received a sixteen-year prison sentence. He also told them that Manley had an assault conviction in Chambers County, Alabama, from 1971 that was the result of an assault with a knife on a

The blue El Camino owned by Charles Travis Manley. This car was specifically identified by witnesses in intricate detail as being occupied by Vieng Phovixay the last time she was seen alive. This photo was taken by Captain Mike Yeager with the Coweta County Sheriff's Office. *Courtesy of Mike Yeager.*

young woman. Spear went on to tell them that Manley had an ex-wife who had a beauty shop in Moreland very near to where Vieng Phovixay had last been seen. Spear gave them Manley's employment information. Manley was employed as an over-the-road truck driver for Tri-Cities Leasing in LaGrange, Georgia.

Mike Yeager, a sheriff's investigator at the time, went to LaGrange and photographed Manley's vehicle at his place of employment. Manley's vehicle was distinctive and exactly fit descriptions by witnesses who saw Vieng leave the trailer park in such a car with an unknown man.

All this information was turned over to the GBI case agent along with the photograph of Manley's 1975 white over greenish-blue El Camino that had mag wheels, white letter tires and a Rebel flag front license plate.

On November 23, 1987, Agent A.H. Davis contacted Officer Spear, who confirmed the information he had conveyed to the sheriff's office.

For some inexplicable reason, there was never an attempt made to have the witnesses identify the photographed car as the vehicle that was witnessed in the trailer park the day of Vieng's disappearance.

For an equally inexplicable reason, there was never an attempt to contact Manley's ex-wife in regard to the possibility that Manley could have been placed in Moreland on the date of Vieng Phovixay's disappearance.

The most incomprehensible failure of all, however, was that at this time, no one contacted Charles Manley to interview him as to his whereabouts and activities on the day of Vieng's disappearance. According to the file, the only action taken in regard to Manley by the case agent was to order a criminal history on Manley that verified the information given by parole officer Mike Spear.

Considering the nature of his past crimes, coupled with the vehicle and his ties to the Moreland area, I find it inconceivable that Charles Manley was never adequately pursued as a suspect in the disappearance of Vieng Phovixay. The case ground to a halt and was administratively closed two months later by the GBI in January 1988, pending further developments or information.

It would be this course of action, or inaction, that would make the case go cold and allow a dangerous evil to continue to dwell among us.

Chapter 12

A HORRIFIC DISCOVERY

On Wednesday, November 1, 1989, it had been over two years since the disappearance of Vieng Phovixay. This day began as most days did for Roy Leach, finding him just after daylight deep in a remote pine forest in east Alabama or west central Georgia. This particular morning found him in rural Harris County, Georgia, some two and a half miles from Sardis Church Road deep in the pine woods on a tract of timber owned by Evergreen Timberlands Corporation.

Roy was an independent forestry consultant. On this day, he was contracted to Evergreen to mark select cut timber for harvesting. The tract he was on encompassed several hundred acres. His job was to methodically traverse the land and identify and mark all the trees that met the criteria to be harvested by the logging crews that would follow over the next few weeks.

The work was meticulous and required much attention to detail. Roy had years of experience cruising timber, and to him, it was a labor of love. Roy was a student of the forest and was constantly aware of changes in the forest around him. At around two o'clock, he noticed a bulge in the pine straw on the ground. He probed the mound of straw with his foot and, to his horror, uncovered what he immediately recognized as a human skull. He began to look around and could see what he believed to be other skeletal remains scattered about.

He returned to his truck, drove back to town, found a phone and called Evergreen Timberlands officials to advise them of his findings on their

Agent Gary Rothwell at the scene where Vieng Phovixay's body was recovered. She was bound to the tree on which Rothwell has his hand. *Courtesy of Gary Rothwell.*

property. He then contacted the Harris County Sheriff's Office to report what he had found.

Upon being advised of the situation, Sheriff John Adams called for assistance from the Georgia Bureau of Investigation. Agent Gary Rothwell contacted Sheriff Adams, and after a discussion of the situation, they decided to wait until the next morning to go to the scene, since by that time darkness was falling and such a remote spot could not be properly investigated in the dark.

Leach was advised not to speak to anyone else about his discovery, as publicity could possibly hinder the efforts of the investigation. All involved agreed to meet the next morning at 8:30 a.m. at the intersection of Monument Road and Sardis Church Road.

Agent Rothwell, Department of Forensic Sciences analyst Bennie Blankenship, Sheriff Adams and Harris County Sheriff's Department major Doug Martin met with Roy Leach and Troy Walker of the Evergreen Timberlands Corporation at the prescribed time and location. From there, Leach led them to a gate at the intersection of Sardis Church Road and Yates Church Road. The gate was secured with a padlock. Sheriff Adams cut the lock, and they proceeded down a clay timber road for approximately one and a half miles and then turned onto a logging road for another 150 yards and stopped their vehicles.

Leach led them to a place approximately fifty yards from the logging road, where he pointed to what was obviously a human skull on the ground. The skull was upright. There was no tissue or jawbone attached to the skull, and it was obvious that it had been there for a long time.

Agent Rothwell at that point organized a systematic search of the area in an effort to locate any other skeletal remains and evidence that might be present. Much of the skeleton as well as articles and scraps of clothing were found in an area some fifty yards long and twenty yards wide. Inside the area was a pine tree with what appeared to be parts of a human spinal column attached to the trunk with strips of cloth similar to the scraps of clothing that had been located at the scene. At this point, it was obvious to Agent Rothwell that this was the scene of a homicide. They proceeded to gather the remains and all evidence at the scene, carefully identifying each piece and charting its location. The trunk of the tree was sawed down and taken intact with the attached strips that had been used to bind the victim. There had been obvious animal activity that had resulted in the scattering of the remains and damage to some of the skeletal remains.

The articles of clothing were a cotton blouse, green pants, a pullover sweater and a pair of panties. Strips of cloth cut from the pants appeared to have been used as bindings to tie the victim to the trunk of the tree. There were corresponding slits in the blouse and sweater that could have resulted from stab wounds to the chest area.

The remains were taken to the crime lab for examination, and Sheriff Adams and his team immediately set about contacting surrounding jurisdictions to see if any missing persons reports existed that might lead to the identification of the victim. With the appeal to the surrounding agencies, several reports were identified as being subject to investigation; however, each of those was quickly ruled out as a possibility.

The following day, November 3, 1989, Dr. Thomas Young, MD, a pathologist employed by the Georgia Bureau of Investigation Division of Forensic Sciences Crime Laboratory, conducted an examination. It was hoped that the information garnered from the examination might shed some light on the identity of the victim and a possible cause of death.

Dr. Young's examination revealed the victim was probably a Caucasian or Asian female, very slight and delicate in build, no greater than five feet in height. The victim was believed to be in her late teens or early twenties. Of the skeletal remains that were recovered, some showed signs of animal activity, and some of the bones were missing.

Dr. Young could find no signs of trauma on the remains that were recovered, but due to the circumstances surrounding the discovery and the remains being bound to a tree, he made the determination that the death was due to homicide. He concluded that the cause of death was undetermined but noted that it was entirely possible that the specific injuries that caused the death would not be present on the skeletonized remains.

Rothwell would leave no stone unturned in his search for the identity of the remains of the woman known at this time only as Jane Doe. He would do everything he could to find those responsible for this heinous crime. He knew that this poor soul had suffered an agonizing and torturous death at the hands of an unspeakable evil that dwelled among us.

Chapter 13

DOWN THE PATH
UNTRAVELED

The first order of business at this point was to attempt to establish the identity of the victim. The skeletal autopsy established that the victim was an Asian female, most likely in her late teens or early twenties. The condition of the remains indicated that they had been there for a long time, well over a year. The discovery was broadcast statewide over the Law Enforcement Data System in hope that it would generate a lead to the young woman's identity.

Due to the location near Columbus and Fort Benning, Georgia, which was known to have a fairly large Asian population, Agent Rothwell began his search there, but to no avail. There were some missing persons, but none fit the description of Rothwell's Jane Doe. Several days passed with no measurable progress in establishing the young woman's identity.

Rothwell met with Agent Ralph Stone of the Georgia Bureau of Investigation Behavioral Analysis Unit. The unit was responsible for developing psychological profiles of suspects in violent crimes. Stone recollected there being a missing person report from Coweta County a couple of years earlier that involved a young Asian female. Stone said that he felt sure the case had been entered in VICAP (Violent Criminal Apprehension Program). The unit had joined in the investigation, but the case had been long since closed. Stone researched his notes and found that the missing person was Vieng Phovixay.

Rothwell went on to discuss the facts in regard to the circumstances by which the remains were found and their condition. Stone was of the opinion that the victim had most likely been sexually assaulted and killed at the location where the remains had been found and that the weapon used was probably a knife. Stone further stated that he felt the person responsible lived near where the remains were found or was familiar with that location.

Armed with the information provided by Stone, Rothwell contacted the Coweta County Sheriff's Office, and it was confirmed that they still had an open missing person's case on a young Asian woman who had disappeared two years earlier from the Moreland area of Coweta County. She fit the physical description of the skeletal remains found in Harris County. Rothwell believed that the remains that had been discovered could possibly be those of Vieng Phovixay.

Gary knew that mere speculation as to the identity was not going to be sufficient. He ordered the GBI file on the Phovixay case and began to research possible avenues that could lead to a positive identification. Rothwell contacted the family, and family members identified the articles of clothing as possibly being those of Vieng. From the family, he obtained the names of the doctor and dentist who had exclusively treated Vieng since her arrival in Newnan.

According to the medical examiner, the skeletal remains revealed perfect teeth with no fillings or cavities, which was consistent with what Rothwell was told by the dentist who had treated Vieng. The skeletal remains showed no sign of healed fractures or deformities. The size and features of the remains were also consistent with the information obtained from Vieng's family physician. While the condition of the remains held no clue to a specific cause of death, it was noted that in cases such as these, the cause of death is often undetermined.

Lastly, Rothwell contacted the United States Department of Immigration and Naturalization to see if by chance there was anything pertinent in the file of Vieng Phovixay that might solidify the identification of the remains as hers. The only thing noted in the file was that she was healthy and vaccinated upon her entry into the United States.

According to the GBI anthropologist, the remains were in a condition that would be consistent with the length of time from Vieng's disappearance to the discovery of the skeletal remains in Harris County.

Armed with these facts, Rothwell felt sure within reason that the remains were those of Vieng Phovixay. Based on Rothwell's investigation, it would be these facts that would lead the Harris County coroner to issue a death certificate for Vieng Phovixay, with the cause of death being undetermined and the manner of death being homicide.

It would be Gary Rothwell's determination and concern that would ultimately result in my resurrecting this case and holding accountable the evil that dwelled among us.

Chapter 14

A NEW BEGINNING

It was easy enough to be swayed by the opinions of those who knew Vieng—her family, her friends, her pastor and her mentors. Everyone seemed to be of the opinion that her boyfriend, Ken Baker, was the most likely suspect in her disappearance. According to some, as of late their relationship had become tumultuous, and according to a few, Vieng had confided that Baker had been physical and struck her. Those facts coupled with the possibility of an unwanted pregnancy on his part made Ken Baker one who certainly had to be eliminated as being responsible for Vieng's disappearance.

Gary Rothwell, however, would not allow opinion and conjecture to sway him from the evidence as he found it. As soon as the identification was made, Rothwell obtained the original file of the GBI case that had been closed two years prior. After reviewing the file, Agent Rothwell knew that there was significant work to be done on this case. He was especially concerned with the lack of the development of Charles Manley as a suspect after the information that was brought forward by parole officer Mike Spear. He set about to rebuild the case from square one. This would require him to reexamine all aspects of the case, reinterview all the witnesses and reevaluate all pertinent information that had been gathered in the initial investigation. It would be an arduous task but one that Gary Rothwell was determined to see through.

Rothwell started by visiting the Coweta County Sheriff's Office, where he spoke with Captain Mike Yeager. Yeager was asked about being contacted by parole officer Mike Spear. Rothwell felt this was an area that had to be explored.

Yeager stated that he had received a call from Spear about a month after Vieng's disappearance. Spear had said that he had a parolee named Charles Travis Manley, a convicted sex offender who drove a very unique vehicle matching the description given by the news reports regarding Vieng's disappearance. Spear went on to say that Manley matched the physical description of the man last seen in the company of Vieng Phovixay and that Manley had an ex-wife who lived in proximity to where Phovixay was last seen with the man described by witnesses. Yeager was advised that Manley was employed as an over-the-road truck driver by Tri Cities Leasing, a trucking company located in LaGrange, Georgia.

Realizing the possible value of this information, Yeager had gone to Manley's place of employment in LaGrange and covertly taken photographs of his 1975 Chevrolet El Camino. The vehicle appeared to be identical to the one described by witnesses. Yeager also obtained photographs of Manley that appeared to resemble the description of the man in whose company Phovixay was last seen. The photos were taken by the Department of Corrections, and in them Manley was younger and close shaven; all other physical characteristics seemed to be consistent with the descriptions rendered by witnesses.

This information was shared with the GBI agent who was working on the case. Yeager took for granted that this information would be followed up on completely. Agent Davis did in fact contact Spear and obtain copies of Manley's previous convictions for rape, assault and burglary, but inconceivably, no one from the GBI interviewed Manley or his ex-wife at that point. It would be this omission that would strike a death knell to the progress of the case.

When asked about his thoughts on Ken Baker, Yeager said that after an extensive interview with investigator Donnie Payne, in which Baker gave a candid account of the last contact he had with Vieng, coupled with the corroboration of the witnesses to last see Vieng Phovixay, he no longer considered Baker a suspect in her disappearance. Yeager also stated that the fact that Baker had voluntarily taken and passed a polygraph examination with no indication of deception had strengthened his opinion that Baker could be eliminated as a suspect. Rothwell was astounded that this avenue of the investigation concerning the information garnered on Manley had not been followed to either a positive conclusion or the effective elimination of Manley as a suspect. Gary knew at this point that he had to explore this possibility with an open mind but could not ignore that Charles Travis Manley had in his mind become a person of tremendous interest in the disappearance of Vieng Phovixay.

Armed with the information in the case file and with what Yeager had told him, Gary Rothwell set out to rebuild this case that had been inexplicably abandoned two years earlier and to begin a relentless search for the evil that dwelled among us.

Chapter 15

MAN ON A MISSION

Gary Rothwell knew that time was not on his side and that rebuilding this investigation at this point would be an uphill battle. Evidence had become stale; witnesses were scattered. To fix this train wreck would require a tremendous amount of work, and Rothwell set about doing just that. The cruelty of the person responsible for this crime and the apparent suffering inflicted on this innocent young woman drove Rothwell to do all he could to find justice for Vieng Phovixay.

After his initial interview with Captain Yeager, Rothwell knew he needed to begin by re-interviewing all the pertinent witnesses. He knew he needed to follow up with those known to have last seen Vieng Phovixay, those being Darlene Wentz, Johnny Wentz and Kenneth Baker. Rothwell realized that the information provided by parole officer Mike Spear could be a game-changing break in the case.

On Monday, November 6, 1989, Rothwell interviewed Spear. Spear related that he had been the parole officer supervising Charles Travis Manley and that he had contacted the Phovixay investigators with this information in 1987 shortly after Phovixay disappeared. He related that his supervision was a result of Manley being convicted of a burglary charge in Troup County in 1980, for which he had received a sixteen-year prison sentence but had been released to parole after serving six years of that sentence.

Spear went on to say that Manley had been convicted for the rape of a Black teenage girl in 1973, for which he had received a sentence of nine years to serve and was paroled after serving five years in 1978.

Spear also stated that although he did not have any documentation of the event, Manley was reported to have been convicted of an assault with a knife of a young woman and her boyfriend in Chambers County, Alabama, in 1972, which resulted in him being charged with assault and assault with intent to rape.

Spear stated that Manley was approximately six feet tall, weighed 230 pounds and had a pot belly. Spear said Manley had a full beard and dark prescription glasses and drove a 1975 El Camino like the one that had been described in association with Phovixay's disappearance. Spear went on to inform Rothwell that Manley's ex-wife Linda Boettcher had a beauty shop just a short distance from where Vieng Phovixay had last been seen with a man matching Manley's description.

In regard to the original witnesses that Rothwell needed to reinterview, Coweta investigators were collaborating with Rothwell in an attempt to locate the trio. Captain Yeager had contacted some of Baker's relatives and was told Baker had a sister in the Macon, Georgia area and that Baker was thought to be staying with her and working for a construction company there.

Rothwell, in the meantime, made inquiries through GBI's Intelligence Division to the Georgia Department of Labor to hopefully ascertain employment history on Charles Manley and Kenneth Baker.

On Monday, November 13, 1989, Rothwell interviewed Darlene Wentz at her residence at Quail Hollow Trailer Park in Newnan. Wentz's recollection of the events and the description of the man last seen with Vieng and his vehicle were absolutely consistent with her statement from 1987 at the time of Vieng's disappearance. One additional item she did recollect, of which there was no mention in the original case file, was that the man with Vieng was drinking a Budweiser beer.

Rothwell's employment inquiry proved fruitful. The Labor Department reported that Manley was last reported as working for Tri Cities Leasing in LaGrange, Georgia, and that Kenneth Baker was employed by Turberfield Construction Company of Macon, Georgia. Baker was found to be working at an out-of-state construction site in South Carolina. Arrangements were made for Baker to meet with Rothwell upon his return to Macon.

On January 17, 1990, Agent Rothwell, Agent Gary Fuller, Sheriff John Adams and GBI Department of Forensic Sciences anthropologist Dr. Karen Burns returned to the site of the recovery of the remains of Vieng Phovixay. The reason for the return to the crime scene was to use anthropological techniques and tools to further process the crime scene.

25 CENTS PER COPY   22 PAGES—ONE S

From left: GBI Agent Gary Fuller and Troup County sheriff's investigators Mike Newsome and Kenneth Reed examine the car of a woman who was kidnapped and sexually assaulted after she stopped the vehicle on Interstate 85 south of LaGrange early Wednesday. The investigators asked that anyone who saw an older model, maroon pickup truck in the vicinity to contact the sheriff's department. (Photo by Larry Fincher)

Police Seek Suspect In Abduction, Rape

A man convinced a 32-year-old woman there was something wrong with her car and when she stopped to investigate, he kidnapped and sexually assaulted her, according to Troup County Sheriff's Investigator Kenneth Reed.

Reed said the woman, who lives in Alpharetta, was travel-

woods and not turn around.

He fled the scene and the victim, whose name was being withheld, walked about a mile along a dirt road before coming to Stovall Road where a motorist stopped and took her to a telephone. She called the Meriwether County Sheriff's Department.

The woman had been visiting

Agent Gary Fuller of the Georgia Bureau of Investigation and investigators Mike Newsome and Ken Reed examine the car belonging to Manley's next victim ten days after the murder of Vieng Phovixay. *Courtesy of Troup County Archives.*

The ground at the base of the pine tree where most of the skeletal remains were found was mulched and sifted. Several small human bones were located, along with one shell-shaped earring without a back. The tree itself was approximately ten inches in diameter and was located about forty yards from the access road. The trunk of the tree was examined and found to have blueish-green treads embedded in the bark approximately two and a half feet from its base.

Dr. Burns removed the soil at the base of the tree down to the clay, which revealed staining that, according to Dr. Burns, was consistent with decomposition of a once living body. Dr. Burns stated that in her opinion, the victim had decomposed at the base of the tree. The sifting process also resulted in the recovery of several strands of human hair.

All the additional evidence was collected and inventoried by Dr. Burns to be taken to the crime lab for further analysis. A four-foot section of the tree trunk containing the fibers was also taken into evidence. After the investigators carefully examined a fifty-yard radius surrounding the tree, the search was concluded.

On Wednesday, February 7, 1990, Agent Rothwell and Sheriff John Adams interviewed Kenneth Baker at his residence, 3044 Bloomfield Drive, Macon, Georgia. Baker was believed to be the last person aside from the murderer to see Vieng Phovixay alive.

Baker stated that he and Phovixay went to high school together and met through mutual friends in 1985. He said that sometime around March 1986, they began dating, and that the relationship became serious in mid-1986. Baker moved in with the Phovixay family in August 1987 and stayed for short while; then he and Vieng moved into their own trailer in the Arnco-Sargent Community of Coweta County. Baker went on to say that after about two months, he and Phovixay broke up over financial problems around the last of September or the first of October 1987, and he moved in with a friend, David Stamey, in the Moreland Trailer Park in Moreland.

Baker's statement mirrored that which he had given in 1987, that Vieng had come to his residence and they talked about the possibility of her being pregnant. Baker said he told her if she was, he'd pay for an abortion or would help raise the child. He went on to say that Vieng was upset and left. A short while later, she returned with the man previously described in the 1987 statement. He stated that the man said he would try to find a tire and come back to help repair Vieng's car. He then left, and a short time later, he returned and said he had a tire if Vieng still wanted him to help her.

Baker stated that he asked Vieng if she wanted to accept the offer of help and accompany the man back to the car, and she indicated that she did. Baker said she got into the El Camino with the man, and they drove away. That was the last time he ever saw Vieng Phovixay.

Rothwell felt confident that with the information furnished by Spear and the solidity of the witnesses' statements, Charles Travis Manley had now become the focus of his investigation. Could he be the evil that dwelled among us?

Chapter 16

SLEEPLESS NIGHTS

I n my years of law enforcement, I've been blessed to have worked and been associated with some tremendously dedicated people, none more so than Gary Rothwell. Our careers somewhat paralleled each other, and on several occasions, I had the pleasure and privilege to work with Gary. Gary was a special agent with the Georgia Bureau of Investigation working out of the Region Two office in Thomaston, Georgia, when I first met him. He was intelligent, hardworking and thorough. He was also compassionate and dedicated to seeking justice.

It would be through my contact with Gary that I would find myself in a quest with him to find justice for Vieng Phovixay. In 2004, I had picked up the 1990 cold case murder of a young man from Troup County. Paul McKeen Jr. had been beaten and left for dead on Georgia Highway 190 in Meriwether County atop Pine Mountain. Oddly enough, Gary had been called as a witness in that trial by the defense, as he had been involved in the original investigation of the McKeen case. The hope of the defense was that there would be facts to come out at trial that contradicted some results in the original case; that, however, didn't happen, and Gary was never called to the stand. Call it what you will, an act of God, providence or just dumb luck; the truth is that that meeting led to some life-altering events for myself, Gary Rothwell and all those concerned in seeking justice for an innocent young woman callously stolen away, tortured and murdered.

I had been blessed with some remarkable success with cold cases. As Gary and I sat on a bench outside the courtroom of the Harris County

Courthouse in April 2005 awaiting a jury verdict on the McKeen case, Gary inquired how it was that we as members of the district attorney's office from the Coweta Judicial Circuit were there prosecuting a murder case in Harris County, which was in the Chattahoochee Judicial Circuit. Until he received that subpoena, Gary had no idea that we had reopened the McKeen case.

I told Gary that I had been told of the case by a mutual friend, Walt Davis, also a special agent with the GBI. Walt and I had begun our careers together with the Georgia State Patrol in the early 1970s. Walt, like Gary, was a good investigator and would go the extra mile to see that justice was served. Walt felt that the case had never been brought to a successful conclusion for several reasons but always felt it could, with more work, be developed to a prosecutable position. I related that the victim, a resident of the Coweta Circuit, had been found gravely injured in Meriwether County, also in the Coweta Circuit; therefore, the investigation began as a Meriwether County case in the Coweta Circuit. After I got the case some fourteen years later, I developed credible evidence that the crime initially began in Harris County in the Chattahoochee Circuit and that it was very likely that the injuries inflicted on the victim that resulted in his death actually occurred in Harris County.

I had the pleasure of working for Coweta Circuit district attorney Pete Skandalakis. Pete was not one to shy away from a case based on difficulty or the time that the investigation would take to put a case together, as long as there was evidence to support going forward. Pete would always listen to what I thought we had in the way of evidence and if I thought there was a reasonable possibility that the case could be brought back to life.

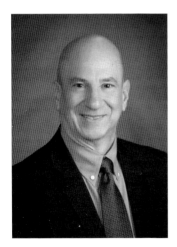

Pete Skandalakis, district attorney of the Coweta Judicial Circuit. *Courtesy of Pete Skandalakis.*

With these jurisdictional questions in mind, and driven by an equal desire to see justice done, District Attorneys Pete Skandalakis and Gray Conger got together and decided that the case should be tried in Harris County. Coweta Circuit district attorney Skandalakis's office, being more familiar with the case, as well as the fact that it was our investigation that had brought the case to a prosecutable conclusion, was invited to try the case as special prosecutors by Chattahoochee Circuit district attorney Gray Conger. This resulted in a case of cooperation between the two that enabled us to find justice for Paul McKeen Jr. and his family.

As I explained to Gary how all this had come about, he began to realize that he had been involved in a situation that just might fall into the same category. I could tell that Gary was excited when he exclaimed, "Well, let me tell you about a case." He went on to say that to that day he still lost sleep over this case.

He then began to tell me of the tragic 1987 case of Vieng Phovixay. Vieng had disappeared from Coweta County in the Coweta Judicial Circuit. Her remains were found two years later tied to a tree in Harris County in the Chattahoochee Judicial Circuit. The case had been inexplicably administratively closed in 1988, only a few months after her disappearance, pending new leads or information. The reason given was that there was no good evidence to continue forward. The case then went cold. This all happened before Gary became involved in the case.

In the fall of 1989, Gary became involved and acutely aware of the shortcomings of the Phovixay investigation. He would embark on a nearly two-year quest for justice for Vieng Phovixay, only to have his efforts cut short by the reluctance of a prosecutor and then by his promotion and transfer, allowing the case once again to be reassigned and fall through the cracks. It would be the conscience and dedication of Gary Rothwell that would again allow me to breathe new life into the case. We would seek justice for Vieng and her family. In our quest for justice, I would discover just how costly to others the failure of the justice system had been. Justice had to be served on that evil that dwelled among us.

Chapter 17

NO STONE LEFT UNTURNED

The tragedy of the Phovixay case haunted Rothwell. While he wanted to devote all his time and resources to bringing Vieng's killer to justice, the truth was he could not. It was during this time that he was also involved in not one but two capital murder cases in Harris County, as well as thirty or so open cases of different degrees that were assigned to him. The Phovixay case, even though it was now open because of its age and condition, would have to be worked on when possible, amid all the others. It, however, would not be neglected, as Gary had developed a strong connection to the case and felt outrage that the animal responsible for this horrific act had not been brought to justice.

Gary methodically set about patiently collecting as much evidence as he could to support the case. The El Camino could still hold vital evidence and needed to be found. Rothwell secured the vehicle identification number from the Troup County tax commissioner's office. It was checked through the Georgia and Alabama Departments of Revenue in hopes of locating the vehicle. The Alabama Department of Revenue had a title application record where title was applied for on a 1975 Chevrolet El Camino by Heyward Cook of Valley, Alabama. It bore the same vehicle identification number as the one that had been registered to Charles Manley in Troup County, Georgia.

On Friday, September 1, 1990, Rothwell conducted an initial voluntary interview with Charles Manley. During this interview, when asked about his ex-wife living in Moreland and if he sometimes visited her there, Manley acknowledged he had on several occasions visited her in Moreland but denied any involvement with Phovixay, as well as denying being in Moreland on the day Phovixay disappeared.

Manley went on to tell Rothwell that he was employed as an over-the-road truck driver by Con Trans Transportation and that his truck was based out of and parked at the Ryder Transportation Shop on Whitesville Road in LaGrange, Georgia. Manley offered to sign waivers to allow voluntary searches of his truck and residence. He also agreed to take a polygraph examination the next day.

On September 2, 1990, Agent Rothwell obtained a search warrant for Manley's residence located on Cannonville Road in LaGrange. The location was searched, and several items were seized in hopes that they would have some probative value in the Phovixay case.

Agents also searched the 1987 Kenworth tractor located at the Ryder Shop in LaGrange that Manley was currently driving. It was found out, however, that he had gotten that truck only in the last couple of weeks, as his regular truck had been involved in an accident and had been replaced.

On September 3, Manley was administered a polygraph examination by GBI agent Thomas Davis of the Polygraph Services Unit. Based on the polygraph chart recordings, it was the opinion of the polygraphist that the physiological responses that are usually indicative of deception were noted when Manley was asked relevant questions regarding the disappearance and murder of Vieng Phovixay.

As the investigation continued on September 8, 1990, Rothwell conducted a most telling interview with Manley's ex-wife Linda Boettcher. It would be this interview that would confirm to Rothwell that he was on the right track to find justice for Vieng. Boettcher told Rothwell that on about Thursday, October 15, 1987, she had learned of the disappearance of a "Vietnamese girl" from the Moreland area the previous Saturday. She stated the newspaper article provided a description of a possible suspect and his vehicle, a Chevrolet El Camino.

Boettcher recalled that on that Saturday morning between ten and eleven o'clock, she saw her ex-husband drive around the block where her beauty shop was located about three times. She knew Manley and she knew his vehicle, a greenish dark El Camino, and there was no doubt it was him. She went on to say Manley had come to her beauty shop before to harass her, threatening to break up her marriage to her current husband. This went on for over a year, but after that day, she never saw or heard from Manley again.

Boettcher told Rothwell that Manley was sick and perverted, that he was obsessed with oral and anal sex and had wanted her to act out acts of sexual bondage. According to Boettcher, she divorced Manley because of his brutality, stating that on several occasions he had beaten her with his fists. Boettcher said after she had divorced Manley, she had let him come to her home, where he raped her the night before he committed the burglary for which he was again sentenced to prison. She said because she had allowed him to come to her house, she didn't think it would do any good to report the rape. Boettcher went on to say that she felt that Manley was fully capable of committing murder.

On September 12, 1990, Rothwell obtained a search warrant issued by R.M. Harper, the magistrate judge of Lee County, Alabama, for the search and seizure of the 1975 Chevrolet El Camino that had once belonged to murder suspect Charles Manley. The warrant was executed at 3068 Lee Road 380, and the vehicle was seized and taken to the Lee County Law Enforcement Center, where it was processed by Agent Rothwell and Agent David Mitchell.

Charles Travis Manley's El Camino, painted black after an attempt to disguise its unique appearance as described by witnesses was made public. *Courtesy of Clay Bryant private collection.*

The search resulted in several pieces of potential evidence, but none proved to have any evidentiary value. The most telling fact was the vehicle itself, which had been amateurishly painted black over what had been a unique and classically appearing vehicle. The striping and emblems had been just painted over in what was an obvious attempt to quickly change the appearance of the vehicle.

Gloria Gay Thornton, another ex-wife of Charles Manley, was interviewed by Agent Rothwell on September 17, 1990. Thornton stated that she had married Manley in December 1985 and divorced him in September 1987, one month prior to the disappearance of Vieng Phovixay.

Thornton described Manley as a very violent man who often beat and intimidated her. On one occasion, after coming home and telling her he had sex with another woman, he forcibly raped her. She stated that he demanded sex, which she refused, and he began to beat her. She picked up a kitchen knife to defend herself. The situation calmed down, and she put the knife down and went into the bathroom to wash her face. Manley approached her from behind, placing the knife to her throat, and told her he'd kill her if she didn't have sex with him, which she did.

Thornton described Manley as a sexually perverted demon who preferred anal sex over any other type of intercourse. She stated that alcohol or drugs caused him to become a Mr. Hyde, and that if he were under the influence of alcohol, she had no doubt he was fully capable of raping and killing a woman.

Kenneth Baker, while being very specific in his descriptions of the suspect and the vehicle during the course of the investigation, had been unable to positively pick the suspect Manley from a photographic lineup. One has to consider that more than two years passed before he was shown the photos, and he actually pointed out Manley as the one most resembling the man he had seen with Vieng. Still, he could not say with moral certainty that the photo was of the man.

Hoping to be able to procure a positive identification on Manley, Rothwell got Ken Baker to agree to be hypnotized, on the chance that hypnosis might jar Baker's subconscious memory and allow him to make a positive identification.

On Tuesday, August 6, Rothwell accompanied Baker to meet with Agent Bob Ingram of the GBI crime analysis unit. Ingram put Baker under hypnosis with the belief that during the session, he would recall details that were not recalled during previous interviews and after which he could likely make a positive identification either from a photo or physical lineup. Unfortunately, few details emerged from the hypnosis session that were beneficial to the case, and when presented with a photo lineup, Baker was once again unable to make an ID with 100 percent certainty.

There comes a moment in all cases when, as they say, it's time to fish or cut bait. The case was now three years old, and while there was no direct evidence connecting Manley to Phovixay, there was a mountain of circumstantial evidence and similar circumstance. For instance, Manley's insistence that he had not been in Moreland at the time of the abduction was clearly refuted by the statement of his ex-wife Linda Boettcher. The vehicle was painted immediately after news reports of its description. All this and more would lead anyone to believe this case was not only indictable but also had a strong possibility of conviction.

During the long course of his investigation, Rothwell stayed in contact with Chattahoochee Circuit district attorney Doug Pullen, keeping him apprised of the progress of the case. The case file was presented to Pullen, but due to the fact that his office was already in the process of prosecuting two capital murder cases, he was reluctant to present it to a grand jury for indictment at that time. Another possible death penalty case would have stretched his office's resources impossibly thin. He wanted to wait until the case was further developed in the hope of producing direct evidence tying Manley to the murder.

At this point, Rothwell had done all he could. He had spent the better part of two years reviving the case to a point where he felt it was in trial-ready condition. Shortly after his presentation of the case for indictment, Agent Gary Rothwell was promoted and transferred as special agent in charge in Perry.

The case of Vieng Phovixay was once again reassigned and relegated to die a slow death. The case later fell into the hands of Agent Lanny Cox, a very capable and respected agent. Upon his review of the case file, he found it to be ripe for prosecution. Cox once again contacted District Attorney Pullen. Cox was told that Rothwell had kept Pullen informed about the progress of the case and was therefore familiar with the facts of the case and the suspect Charles Manley. Pullen stated that he had known Manley and his family personally for many years.

Pullen did not see the need to have a copy of the case file sent to his office unless new evidence was developed in the case. At least for the time being, this effectively ended the quest to bring the evil that dwelled among us to justice.

Chapter 18

THE REVIVAL

During my tenure as an investigator in the Coweta Judicial Circuit in west central Georgia, I worked for district attorney Pete Skandalakis. I was privileged to work for a man who was truly a justice-seeking individual. He was not afraid to invest time and resources in cases that had long been abandoned, provided I could convince him more work could potentially breathe new life back into the case and that there was a possibility of justice being served.

Pete and I had developed a history with cold cases; our success in dealing with them was nothing short of phenomenal. In just a three-year period, we solved four, the oldest being thirty-three years old and the most recent fourteen. All resulted in positive outcomes. Pete allowed me a free hand in dealing with cold cases as long as it didn't interfere with my other day-to-day duties in the office.

After what Gary had told me about the Phovixay case, I knew I had to go to Pete and get his blessing to delve into the matter. I was absolutely sure Pete would be all in; he wasn't afraid to tackle a tough case in order to find justice for a victim. I knew from talking with Gary that he felt a grave injustice needed to be made right; that alone was enough for me, and I was sure it would be enough for Pete as well.

I went to Pete and relayed the story that Gary had told me. After hearing my take on the situation, Pete, as I knew he would, allowed me to get the old case file from the GBI so we could look at it. Our initial thought was that the kidnapping had occurred in our circuit and that gave us the grounds we needed to justify reopening the investigation.

After my request, within a few days I had the file in hand. With great anticipation, I read it from cover to cover. It was just as Gary had described. The initial investigation appeared to be sorely inadequate; when new and pertinent facts had come forward, they had never been acted on. From the time that Phovixay's remains were found, however, the investigation appeared to me to be thorough and complete. With the work that had been put into the case and with what appeared to be a mountain of similar circumstance and circumstantial evidence, I could not imagine in what world this case had not been indicted.

After I went over the file with Pete, it was apparent to both of us that this case could and should have been brought to a just conclusion. The work that Rothwell had done after the body was found was stellar. To refresh the case would be a daunting task but not an impossible one.

I contacted Gary and told him the news that we were going to reopen the investigation. Gary was excited for the opportunity to once again be on the hunt for justice for Vieng Phovixay. Gary at this time was the special agent in charge of the GBI regional office in Perry, Georgia, so his in-person help was going to be limited; he did, however, agree to give all the assistance that he could.

I was ecstatic. I felt that with some work, we were going to be able to obtain a just result. There was no greater accomplishment to me than to be able to right a long-standing wrong. Vieng Phovixay and her family surely deserved the answers to the questions that they had long been deprived of.

I knew full well the difficulties that we faced. Witnesses and victims had to be located and contacted. Evidence had to be retrieved, if it still existed. As difficult as the task was going to be, to me it was going to be a labor of love. I would find great satisfaction in bringing to justice and expelling that terrible evil that dwelled among us.

Chapter 19

TIME IS NOT YOUR FRIEND

S o-called cold cases are cold for a reason. In the Phovixay case, no information or evidence had come forward to bring about a positive resolution to the case. When you are revisiting a cold case, time is not and has not been your friend. In time, witnesses become lost or, worse, die; memories fade; and evidence is misplaced, lost or destroyed. Time alone can become the greatest obstacle that has to be overcome in order to salvage a case that has gone cold.

Conversely, time on occasion can be an asset; sometimes witnesses find that their fear of becoming involved fades with time. Witnesses' morals and values sometimes change with age, and this can result in their coming forward with information that in times past they were reluctant to provide for whatever reason.

The first order of business in this quest for answers was to locate the initial witnesses. One has to understand that in this case, seventeen years had passed since these people had been contacted, and people go on living their lives. They move to new locations; they marry, divorce, remarry; some just don't want to be found; and unfortunately, some die. This case contained all these obstacles, but in the search for justice for Vieng Phovixay, I was bound to adapt and overcome these obstacles.

I worked out of the Troup County office of the Coweta Judicial Circuit, and most of the people I needed to find were last known to live in the Newnan area of Coweta County. I enlisted my counterpart, Investigator Bob Lines of the Coweta County office, to assist me in this critical task. Unfortunately,

I am extremely old school; investigation to me is mostly face to face, one on one. We at the district attorney's office were provided with the latest and greatest in technology. My problem was that I was about as computer savvy as a brick; Bob, on the other hand, was a LexisNexis guru. LexisNexis is an advanced people-locating computer program. It can locate anyone who has ever left any kind of paper trail; it will locate you and can find your relatives, neighbors or business associates. Locating people is difficult enough; getting them to tell you what they honestly know is another whole level of difficulty.

Between Bob and me, we were able to locate every witness and victim with the exception of Manley's second wife, as she had passed away a year prior. I was also unable to find any arrest or court records of the assault on the couple in Chambers County, Alabama, which would identify and locate the couple that parole officer Mike Spear reported Manley had assaulted in the early '70s and that he had been unable to document. This similar circumstance would be vital to our case. The search for these victims would continue.

I also began to try to locate any physical evidence that had not been destroyed. I felt sure this was a long shot at best. I contacted Gary Rothwell to elicit his help with this task. To my amazement, Gary was able to locate all the evidence recovered in the Phovixay case, including the section of the pine tree to which she had been bound.

I was of the opinion that Gary Rothwell had drawn a pretty good map to carry us to a successful conclusion to solving the murder of Vieng Phovixay. But it was going to take some legwork. There were a lot of dots that had to be reconnected. I reported the progress to Pete Skandalakis on nearly a daily basis. He was as excited as I was at the possibility that we would be able to convict Vieng's killer and bring some closure to Vieng's family and those who loved her.

There was still a significant question to be answered regarding venue in the case. Venue is determined by the location in which a crime is committed. Georgia law states that a crime is to be tried in the county in which the crime is committed. The kidnapping of Vieng was initiated in Coweta County in our judicial circuit, but the evidence showed that the murder and a continuation of the initial crime was in Harris County in the Chattahoochee Circuit.

In the recent past, Pete and Gray Conger, the district attorney in the Chattahoochee Circuit, had collaborated on a murder case that I had brought, and we were invited as special prosecutors to try the case in Harris County. This had resulted in three defendants being convicted in the 1992 cold case murder of Paul McKeen Jr.

Once again, the cooperation between the two district attorneys was instrumental in the case moving forward. We were again invited in as special prosecutors in the Chattahoochee Circuit. Pete appointed Ray Mayer to be the lead prosecutor in the case. Ray had gotten convictions in the McKeen case, and I was delighted that I would be working with him again. Ray was an excellent prosecutor. I have had the honor and pleasure to work with many good prosecuting attorneys, and he was one of the very best. From this point forward, Ray would be in charge of the prosecutorial decisions in the case, and I knew it couldn't have been in better hands.

It appeared we were well on our way to rebuilding a case that hopefully would expose and bring to justice the evil that dwelled among us.

Chapter 20

IN GOD'S TIME

I have never been one to believe in the supernatural; however, I do believe that God sometimes works in mysterious ways that we don't understand and cannot explain. I do believe that God works through people to achieve his will. Throughout my experience in investigating cold cases, many times I have come to an impasse that I was absolutely sure would end the quest for the truth. Then, by some inexplicable circumstance, a door would open that would result in a revival of the case and ultimately a resolution that found the long-deserved justice for the victims and their families.

My only answer for this is that God delivered the answers that I needed in his time. I have come to be a true believer that through people he has chosen, God works in God's time. In my experience, there has never been a greater example of this than in the case of Vieng Phovixay.

When trying to find the dirt, so to speak, on a man, oftentimes you need go no further than his ex-girlfriends and ex-wives to discover what he is capable of. Such was the case with Charles Travis Manley. In an interview with his most recent ex-wife, Gloria Manley Bryan, I was enlightened to just how depraved he was. She related facts and circumstances that were shocking to say the least, and she was very afraid of him to that day. It was during this conversation that she related to me that he had been found guilty of a sexual assault in Chambers County, Alabama, in the early '70s. This had to be the incident that Mike Spear had reported in 1987, but so far, I had found no mention of it in Manley's criminal history. Knowing that this would be valuable to the case as a similar circumstance, if in fact it had occurred, I immediately began to try to find it.

I began with the clerk of court in Chambers County, but there was no felony record of such a case on file. Gloria Manley Bryan had given specifics of the crime but did not know the victim's name. I felt she possibly had not been correct on the location of the incident, so I checked all the surrounding counties for the case, but to no avail. The case at this point was coming together nicely, but if in fact this incident had occurred, it would bolster our case tremendously. A few weeks passed without any further information about this incident.

I continued to research Manley's past relationships and requested any divorce cases to which he was a party on file with the Troup County clerk of court, where Manley had continued to reside. Melanie Bowles, the deputy clerk over civil matters, agreed to research the cases on file that involved Manley.

A few days passed before my wife, who was a deputy clerk of the Troup County Superior Court, called me in the afternoon and asked if I would like to meet with her and some of the other ladies from the clerk's office at a local restaurant for a drink and dinner. I of course replied that I would meet them there. When I arrived, everyone was already there and seated at a table, where I joined them.

I knew everyone at the table with the exception of one woman. I was immediately introduced to her as the sister-in-law of one of the girls from the clerk's office. I had never met or seen this woman before. She was pleasant and introduced herself as Betty Moore.

As we all sat and were involved in conversation, Melanie spoke to me and said that she had the information I wanted on Charles Travis Manley. She told me she had it all copied and that I could pick it up the next day. I told her I'd stop by the next morning and pick it up.

I had seen several people whom I knew seated in the dining room and proceeded to go speak to them. As I was walking back to our table, the sister-in-law met me and asked abruptly why we had mentioned Manley. I replied to her that I was investigating a serious crime that he may have had some involvement in. She looked me straight in the eye and in a solemn voice said, "He assaulted me in 1971." She then went on to relate some vague details of the incident. I began to realize that this woman was the victim of the incident that I had been searching for all over east Alabama and west central Georgia. She agreed to being interviewed the next day.

I met with her, and she related to me that in 1971, she and her boyfriend were accosted at knifepoint. Manley held a knife to her throat as he attempted to force her boyfriend into the trunk of their car. Manley made clear his intentions were to sexually assault her. As Manley was attempting to assault her, she was able to knee him in the groin, resulting in his turning her loose. She was able to separate herself from him enough to get to the opposite side of the car, and Manley was unable to overtake her again. After seeing he wasn't going to be able to regain his control over her, he told her that if she reported what had happened, he would kill them. They immediately reported the incident, and Manley was promptly arrested and charged with two counts of aggravated assault and assault with intent to rape.

Manley subsequently pleaded guilty in open court in Chambers County and was awaiting sentencing. Inexplicably, a short time later, he was allowed to come back before the judge and withdraw his plea of guilty to the previous charges and, per a plea agreement, plead guilty to one count of misdemeanor assault and battery outside the presence of the victims. He was subsequently fined $125, sentenced to time served and released.

After extensively searching for a record of this crime and its victim with absolutely no luck at all, I found myself sitting across from a woman at a restaurant who, with only the mention of a name, raised the issue. It was inconceivable that this could happen. Even more unbelievable was the fact that this discovery came on the day before I was to begin interviewing the witnesses we had been able to locate. I could only attribute it to my being led to her by a higher power in God's time.

The woman was able to identify her companion when the attack occurred as Roger Garner. Both of them would become similar circumstance witnesses for the prosecution at Manley's trial. They and others like them would ensure that justice would finally be levied on the evil that dwelled among us.

Chapter 21

RETRACING STEPS
FROM THE PAST

April 1, 2005, marked the next step in finding justice for Vieng Phovixay. It was time to begin to interview all the factual and similar circumstance witnesses to assess the value and validity of their testimony. As I have stated before, time dims the memory and recall begins to fade. There are certain circumstances, however, that can mitigate this. There are memories that are forever implanted in the conscious and subconscious of a person. I call these landmark memories. If I simply gave you a date and asked you to recall an everyday event that happened on June 12, 2010, it would be all but impossible.

I would, however, be willing to wager that if I asked you where you were and what you were doing on September 11, 2001, when you heard about the attack on the New York World Trade Center, you'd be able to recall it precisely. The magnitude of the event burns that memory forever in your mind. The memory of that landmark in time allows a person to hold a thought or mental picture in their mind indefinitely. It was my hope that the events that were associated with Vieng's disappearance were significant enough, especially to those witnesses who had seen the suspect, to trigger that landmark memory.

I began this trip down memory lane with Betty Moore and Roger Garner, whom I'd identified only the day before. They both recounted the events of 1971 in Chambers County, Alabama, just as we had been told. Garner knew Manley and was 100 percent sure he was the perpetrator that had assaulted them.

Next, I spoke with Jerry and Ann George. Jerry recalled being called to Moreland by his sister, Manley's ex-wife Linda Boettcher, on a Saturday morning. Linda had seen Manley circle the block by her beauty shop three or four times. She told Jerry to please come to make sure that if Manley came back he would not start trouble. Jerry did in fact go to Moreland but had no contact with Manley. However, the following week, Boettcher told Jerry of Vieng's disappearance and went on to say that she thought Manley had been responsible. Ann George related a similar story regarding Jerry leaving the house to go to Moreland at his sister's request because of her fear of Manley.

Next on my list to contact was Darlene Wentz, now Boynton. She was one of the witnesses who had actually seen the suspect with Vieng on the day of her disappearance. When she had been shown a lineup by Gary Rothwell that included Manley in 1990, she picked Manley out but said she was not 100 percent sure that it was him. I was willing to risk showing her another lineup that included Manley in hope that her landmark memory would allow her to pick him out. The photo I had was one that showed him with a full beard and dark glasses, just as she had described him back in 1987.

Ray Mayer and I had already discussed the fact that the defense would raise the question as to whether or not I influenced the identification should Boynton pick Manley out of the lineup. To combat that possibility, I had Investigator Lines present at the interview and lineup.

In the interview, Boynton almost identically replicated the story that she gave in 1987 to Allan Davis and again in 1990 to Gary Rothwell. She gave a very specific description of the suspect and the vehicle. When asked if she would look at the lineup, she indicated that she would. The lineup was a six-man standard lineup and contained all males similar in appearance to Manley, with full beard, mustache, glasses and brown hair.

Upon Boynton seeing the lineup, she almost immediately pointed to photo number five and emphatically said, "That's him, that's the man I saw drive away with Vieng." Boynton stated she would testify for the state if need be, and the interview was concluded.

Number five was Charles Travis Manley. I was ecstatic. I reported the results of the interview to Ray, and he was cautiously optimistic, for he realized, as my daddy would say, "We got a ways to go before we know this dog will hunt."

On April 1, 2005, I conducted an interview with Gloria Bryan, another ex-wife of Charles Manley. In the interview, Bryan stated that she had been married to Manley and that their relationship was a tumultuous one. She

The lineup that was used to identify Charles Travis Manley. Manley is listed in picture #5. *Courtesy of Clay Bryant private collection.*

said Manley was a perverted and violent person. She stated that she had been beaten by Manley on numerous occasions. Bryan said Manley habitually smoked marijuana and consumed large amounts of alcohol, which made him verbally and physically abusive. She related one event where she was maritally raped with a knife held to her throat. She said after that incident she divorced Manley. She went on to say that to this day she was terrified of him and was of the opinion he was capable of committing sexual assault and murder.

I showed Bryan a copy of the statement she had given to Agent Rothwell in 1990. She read the statement, and when asked if it was the information given to Rothwell, she stated it was correct and she stood by it. Bryan stated she was willing to testify in court if necessary. The interview was concluded.

On April 12, 2005, I conducted an interview with Gloria Bailey Tyner, the victim of a rape committed by Manley in 1973. Tyner stated that she was fifteen years old at the time it happened. She said a man she knew as

Charles Manley came to her home and said he needed a babysitter and that her grandmother had recommended her. Tyner's grandmother had worked as a maid for Manley's father, and she knew Charles. The grandmother recommended that Tyner take her little sister, who was twelve years old, along with her while she watched the children. They got in the car with Manley. Manley drove up U.S. 29 through West Point, where he lived, turned on Lovelace Road in a remote area and pulled onto a field road.

Manley at that point produced a handgun. The younger girl began to scream. According to Tyner, Manley said if she didn't shut up, he would kill her. Tyner said she was able to calm down her sister, and Manley told her to get out of the car. Manley at that point raped the elder sister at gunpoint, after which he told Tyner he was going to have to kill her. Tyner said she was completely terrified. She felt her only chance was to jump from the car and run. Manley pursued her a short distance and then gave up. Manley had taken her clothes. Tyner said as she walked along the road, she saw headlights approaching and ducked back into the woods as the car that she thought was Manley's passed by.

Tyner continued down the road to a house where a woman summoned help and gave her some clothes. Tyner and her sister were picked up by family members and taken to the West Point police station.

Tyner stated that Manley had pleaded guilty to the charge of rape and was sentenced to prison. She went on to say that she never understood why he was sentenced to only nine years after pleading guilty to what he had done. She indicated she would be glad to testify for the state at trial. The interview was concluded.

I had performed an Auto Trax search in an attempt to locate Johnny Wentz. I was able to obtain an address in Pine Mountain Valley in Harris County, Georgia, along with a phone number. I contacted Wentz, and he agreed for me to come to his home for an interview.

Wentz was one of the only people to have seen Vieng and the suspect together that day. It was my intention to show him photographs in the hope that he could positively identify the suspect or the vehicle. Of course, I knew that once again such an identification would come under attack by the defense. I enlisted Sergeant Rodney Collier of the Harris County Sheriff's Office to accompany me to witness the integrity of the photograph identifications if indeed they were made.

Wentz and his wife at the time had lived on the lot adjacent to the trailer where Ken Baker was living. He stated that he knew Vieng Phovixay and had spoken with her on several occasions. I showed him a photograph of

Vieng and asked him if he knew who this person was. He immediately answered that it was Vieng Phovixay. We spoke further about the case, and Wentz related that he had initially been interviewed at the time of Vieng's disappearance and that he had given a description of the man in the company of Vieng on the day she was last seen and the vehicle he drove. He said the next he heard of the case was when her remains were found a couple of years later.

That morning, Wentz said he had seen Vieng enter the trailer park with a man whom he described as five feet ten inches tall, heavyset, with a beer belly. Wentz said the man also had a full beard and wore dark glasses. He said he thought he recognized him from seeing him in a bar in the area.

Wentz said the car the man was driving was of particular interest to him. He had actually approached the man and spoken to him at length about the vehicle and even asked if the man wanted to sell it. He described the car as a 1975 Chevrolet El Camino, greenish-blue with white SS stripes and a white vinyl top. Wentz said the car had mag wheels and a Rebel flag license plate on the front.

I showed Wentz the picture that Investigator Mike Yeager had covertly taken of Manley's vehicle. He stated, "That's the car, without a doubt that's it." I then asked him if he thought he could identify the man whom he had seen with Vieng. He said he felt sure that he could.

I showed him the lineup that contained a photo of Charles Manley. Wentz pointed to the photo in position five and said, "That's him." I asked Wentz if he was sure. He replied without a doubt, "That's him; I recognize him like it was yesterday." The photo in position five was that of Charles Travis Manley.

Knowing that his ex-wife had already seen the lineup, I asked Wentz if he had spoken to her about the case. Wentz replied that he had not spoken to her in several years and had no idea where she was.

As rebuilding this case proceeded, I could not understand how our justice system, one that I know is not perfect but one that I do believe in, could have gotten this so wrong. It repeatedly allowed so many of those it should have protected to suffer pain and anguish at the hands of the evil that was allowed to dwell among us.

Chapter 22

NEVER-ENDING DEVASTATION

One must wonder just how much pain, suffering and personal tragedy one individual can be responsible for inflicting. In the case of Charles Travis Manley, the answer to that question would seem to be unlimited.

The case had gotten so much into my mind that it pretty much consumed me. I tried to think of every angle I could to develop more credible evidence. In early May 2005, I contacted my good friend and retired GBI agent Gary Fuller. I knew from the case file that Fuller had assisted Rothwell in some aspects of the investigation into Vieng's murder.

As we spoke, I was going over the evidence we had with Gary, and when I was telling him about the positive identifications from the lineup, I alluded to the consistent descriptions given by the witnesses. I told Gary that the suspect at the time of Vieng's disappearance had lived in West Point. Gary's expression changed, and he said, "I remember working a kidnapping and rape somewhere in the mid-'80s in Troup County on Interstate 85 at West Point, and if I'm not mistaken the description of the suspect is very similar to your suspect." Gary recalled that the suspect stopped the woman on the interstate, put a knife to her throat and then took her to a remote area in Meriwether County, where she was viciously raped and sodomized. I felt sure Manley was a viable suspect in this crime as well.

Gary could not be sure of the date, only a wide time frame. I immediately set about trying to locate the reports of this crime with the GBI and the Troup County Sheriff's Office. Because of the wide time span, I was unable to locate the reports with either entity. I then turned to Kaye Minchew at the Troup County Archives; the archives had been so helpful to my investigations in the past that I felt confident they would have some type of record of this incident. They performed a topic search and were able to retrieve a newspaper article from the *LaGrange Daily News* dated October 19, 1987. The incident had taken place the day before on October 18, 1987, just eighteen days after the disappearance of Vieng Phovixay. With this information, I was able to obtain both the GBI and the Troup County case files on the incident.

On the morning of October 18, 1987, Denise Williams left the Holiday Inn in Lanett, Alabama. Unbeknown to her, the wife of Charles Manley was working the desk when she checked out. She turned northbound onto Interstate 85 and crossed into Troup County, Georgia. As she drove, a dark-colored pickup truck pulled alongside her. The driver of the pickup urged the woman to the side of the road. As he approached her car, he was saying there were sparks coming from under her car. As the woman bent down to see if she could see a problem, the man approached from behind and grabbed the young woman and held a knife to her throat.

He forced her into his vehicle and onto the floorboard, telling her that if she tried to escape, he would kill her. The man drove for approximately twenty-five miles to a remote location in Meriwether County, where he repeatedly raped and sodomized Williams. Her clothes and a diamond ring were taken. The rapist began to apologize for the fact that he was going to have to kill her. Williams began to beg for her life, saying she had children whom she needed to be there for.

At that point, the man told her to get out of the truck and start walking toward a distant tree line, and if she looked back, he would kill her. Barefoot and naked, she walked away, fearing any minute he would attack her again and kill her. After walking a good distance, she heard the truck's engine and could hear him drive away.

After waiting hidden for a time, she began walking until she got to a dirt road that led her to a paved road. She stated that at first when she heard a car, she would get off the road, fearing that he had come back. When Williams saw a car that she was sure was not him, she flagged it down and told the people in the car she had been raped. The people in the car told her to get in the car, which she did. They drove to their house nearby and called the police.

As I read the heart-wrenching account of this young woman, I immediately was aware of the many similarities in this case to the cases involving Charles Manley. I felt sure that Manley had to be considered a suspect in this long-unsolved crime.

I set about attempting to locate Williams. I was able to use the information gathered from the reports to locate her in the Birmingham, Alabama area. I contacted the Shelby County, Alabama District Attorney's office; Investigator Mark Hall contacted her on my behalf and advised her that we thought we might have a suspect in her long-forgotten case. I was then able to reach her by phone; I told her that I was investigating another case when I was made aware of similarities between it and the case in which she was a victim. I asked if she thought she could identify her attacker, and she said that she was sure she could.

I enlisted the help of Investigator Kelli Schlader of the Troup County Sheriff's Office as I felt Williams would be more comfortable talking about the incident in the presence of a female officer. Schlader had vast experience investigating sex crimes, and I knew she would be an asset in this investigation.

On June 7, 2005, Schlader and I traveled to Pelham, Alabama, to meet with Williams. She painfully recounted her horrific ordeal. She said that the man had taken her clothes and a ring that her parents had given her when she graduated college. She described the ring and to our amazement had a picture of it on her hand.

We presented her with a lineup of six individuals, and in the presence of Investigator Schlader and her husband, she immediately pointed to the picture of Charles Manley and emphatically said, "That's the man." We went on to tell her about how we had gotten to where we were with the investigation. She thanked us for what we were doing and said that she would testify against Manley in her case and also as a similar circumstance witness in the Phovixay case. Kelli and I said goodbye and that we'd be in touch. We drove back to LaGrange riding a wave of accomplishment, but we still had work to do.

I inquired of the crime lab as to the status of the rape evidence that was collected from Williams; sadly, I was told that the evidence had been destroyed on May 16, 1990, due to the fact that no one had replied to a status inquiry of the case.

At the time this incident occurred, Manley was married to his second wife, Gloria Manley. I called her and asked if she had knowledge of a ring that Charles may have had in his possession. She told me he had given her a ring that he said he had gotten at a flea market. I asked if I could come to her residence and show her the photograph of the ring, and she said she'd be glad to look at the ring. I drove to her residence, where she observed the photo of the ring. Gloria said that appeared to be the ring Charles had given her. She said that she had sold the ring to Valley Pawn Shop years ago, but she recalled the ring well, as it was the only thing Manley had ever given her.

By now, Ray Mayer was excited with the progress that was being made and was beginning to be confident in the case that we could put before a jury. We had just a few more loose ends to tie up before proceeding forward.

On June 20, 2005, Gary Rothwell and I conducted a non-custodial interview with Charles Manley at the GBI Regional Crime Lab in Columbus, Georgia. During this interview, Manley acknowledged his presence in Moreland on the date that Vieng Phovixay went missing. He stated he had gone to Moreland to borrow $200 from his ex-wife, but she would not let him have the money but did agree to have sex with him. When confronted with the descriptions given by witnesses of the man and his vehicle last seen with Phovixay, his answer was that he thought it was a plot by his ex-wife to get him into trouble. He said he had never been to the trailer park in Moreland and never had any contact with Vieng Phovixay. In the interview, he was cold, matter-of-fact and convinced he was untouchable, and he seemed to brag about the fact that he could still have sex with women from his past, using the term "grudge fuck." The interview was concluded, and Manley left.

Gary and I knew that we had enough evidence and witness testimony to present a compelling case to a jury. I wanted to talk to one more witness. On June 22, 2005, I spoke with Roger Thornhill. Thornhill painted Manley's 1975 El Camino in late October 1987 shortly after the news of Vieng's disappearance was aired on Atlanta television news stations, including a detailed description of the vehicle Vieng was last seen in. Thornhill said that Manley brought the car to his shop and wanted to get the car painted with a cheap paint job. He didn't want any normal prep done to the car, not even removing the striping. Thornhill said that he wondered why anyone would do this to a really unique vehicle, but he said he never questioned Manley as to the reason. He said he just complied with Manley's request and sprayed the car black.

We were now at a point where I knew we were closing in, and it was just a matter of time until we would bring to justice the evil that dwelled among us.

Chapter 23

TIME TO GO FISHING

We were at the proverbial point where it was time to "fish or cut bait." Ray Mayer was satisfied that we had done all we could in the way of building a prosecutable case. There does come a time in a case when you know that you have produced everything you can from an evidentiary standpoint. I was confident that we were there.

That's where the value of an excellent prosecutor comes in. He or she anticipates the points that the defense will likely attack. In the case of the remains, there was no dental work identifiable; identification was made from clothing that had been exposed to the elements for two years and from the opinion of the state's medical examiner that this was a female in her twenties of Asian descent.

Ray knew that with the mountain of evidence we had compiled, the defense would raise any question that could put doubt in the mind of a single juror about the validity of our case. That one juror could doom the case to failure. The remains were found over fifty miles from where Vieng was last seen, and there were no dental records or scientific evidence that the remains were those of Vieng Phovixay. Ray anticipated that these facts would be raised as a point of contention; the issue had to be dealt with. This and other issues could be handled in the long wait before trial.

After a roundhouse conference with Pete, Ray, Gary, myself and Harris County district attorney Gray Conger, it was decided it was indeed time to fish, and I had been given the honor of setting the hook.

Columbus Ledger Enquirer newspaper article regarding the abduction and murder of Vieng Phovixay and Charles Travis Manley after Manley's arrest. *Courtesy of* Columbus Ledger Enquirer.

On June 28, 2005, I went before Judge William Smith and obtained a warrant for Charles Travis Manley for the malice murder of Vieng Phovixay. With warrant in hand, the next order of business was to arrange to take Manley into custody.

I contacted Gary Rothwell and told him I had obtained the warrant. I knew that he would surely want to take part in Manley's arrest, since if not for his work and desire to see justice served, this case would not have come to a just resolution.

Manley at this time was driving an over-the-road truck for a company in Columbus, Georgia. I contacted his employer and was told he had just gone out on a long-haul trip and it would be several days before he returned. We decided that our best course of action would be to arrest him immediately upon his return. The employer was advised of the situation and was told that if he would keep us apprised of Manley's whereabouts, we would not cause a disruption to their business and would take Manley into custody upon his return.

On July 12, 2005, I met Gary Rothwell, and we traveled to Manley's place of employment and awaited his return. We had been given his time of arrival. As Charles Manley stepped down from the cab of his truck, Gary and I approached him. I could hardly contain myself as I looked him in the eye and said, "Charles Travis Manley, I have a warrant for your arrest for the murder of Vieng Phovixay." The look on Manley's face was not one of surprise but more of sullen acceptance. Manley was read his Miranda rights, and he quickly invoked his right to an attorney before speaking with us. Gary and I transported Manley to the Harris County Jail in Hamilton, Georgia, where he was booked into the jail for murder.

Gary and I congratulated each other for the successful work that we had done, but we departed knowing that our work was not finished. Gary headed back to Perry and I to LaGrange. As I drove north, I couldn't help but think about the promise of a young life senselessly taken and the nearly twenty years of endless pain and anguish suffered by Vieng's family as they struggled to find answers that weren't to be found. I felt an immense sense of accomplishment, knowing that their prayers for answers were finally being answered. I was proud of the work that we had done and looked forward to completing our mission of holding responsible and convicting the animal who took that young life. There was a great comfort in knowing that justice was getting done and there would finally no longer be a danger posed by the evil that dwelled among us.

Chapter 24

LOOSE ENDS

The work that had to be done on this case was far from ended with the arrest of Charles Manley. There were other issues as well with the other cases against Manley that had to be addressed.

Manley was indicted on September 12, 2005, by the Harris County Grand Jury, charging him with one count of malice murder and one count of felony murder. Manley had employed an exceptionally fine criminal defense attorney from Atlanta. Brian Steele was recognized, and rightfully so, as one of the best criminal defense attorneys in Georgia. Steele brought Ann T. Shafer on as co-counsel. Shafer was also somewhat of a legal legend in criminal defense. Manley would have as good a defense team as anyone could have gotten. This emphasized the need to have every *i* dotted and every *t* crossed, as we were certain that even upon conviction, the prosecution would have to withstand a vigorous appeal process brought by two exceptional legal minds.

First and foremost, the need to solidify the identity of the found remains had to be addressed. The most effective way to lay this issue to rest would be to use mitochondrial DNA. In order to facilitate this, the remains of the victim would have to be exhumed in an attempt to extract a DNA sample to be compared with a family member in the same maternal line as Vieng Phovixay.

The act of exhuming a body is a huge step; it raises religious, moral and emotional concerns of a family already in grief over the situation. Pete Skandalakis always held those concerns of survivors in the highest

The beginning of the exhumation of the body of Vieng Phovixay at the Oak Hill Cemetery in Newnan. *Courtesy of Clay Bryant private collection.*

Exhumation of Vieng Phovixay. *Courtesy of Clay Bryant private collection.*

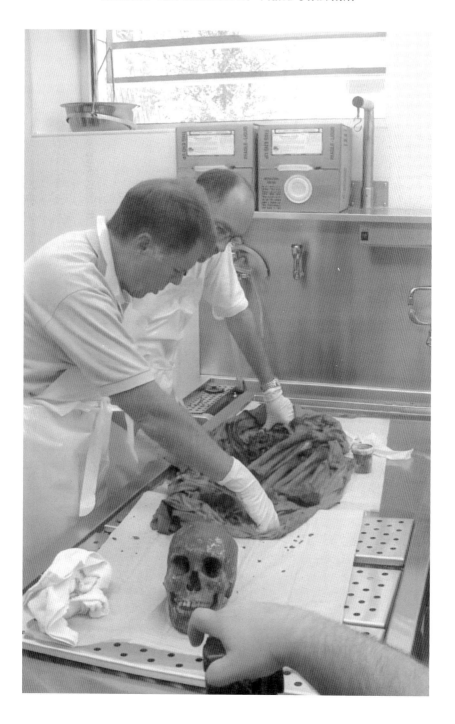

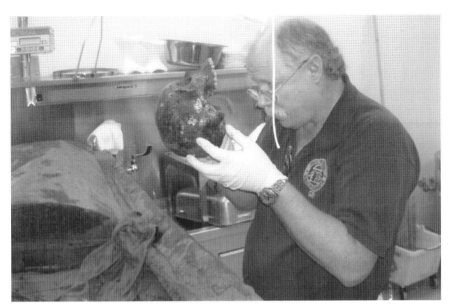

Opposite: Beginning the examination of the remains of Vieng Phovixay by Dr. Kris Sperry and Dr. Fredrick Snow at the Georgia State Crime Lab. Dr. Sperry is the director of the crime lab and the chief medical examiner for the State of Georgia. Dr. Snow is a renowned criminal anthropologist. He at that time was employed by the Georgia Bureau of Investigation Crime Lab. *Courtesy of Clay Bryant private collection.*

This page: Dr. Sperry examines the remains of Vieng Phovixay. *Courtesy of Clay Bryant private collection.*

Dr. Snow examines the remains of Vieng Phovixay at the Georgia State Crime Lab. *Courtesy of Clay Bryant private collection.*

consideration. Phyllis Williams, the victim's advocate on this case, and I contacted the family to get their input as to their wishes on the issue of exhumation. After hearing the potential importance of this exhumation, the family united in agreement that they supported it.

The GBI Crime Lab agreed to do a second autopsy, as now they had a renowned criminal anthropologist, Dr. Fredrick Snow, who would do the skeletal autopsy along with Dr. Kris Sperry. The goal was hopefully to discover further evidence, as well as to extract the necessary DNA to solidify the identity of the victim.

Skandalakis petitioned the court to order the body to be exhumed. That order was issued by Judge Jeanette Little on July 29, 2005. The remains were exhumed from the Oak Hill Cemetery in Newnan, Georgia, and transported to the GBI Crime Lab in Decatur, where the skeletal autopsy was performed. There was no further evidence garnered from the remains in regard to the cause of death. There was DNA extracted from the remains. A DNA sample was given by Amphay Phovixay, Vieng's younger sister. The result of the mitochondrial DNA analysis was that both Amphay and the remains exhumed came from the same mother. Any question as to the identity of the remains was answered; they were those of Vieng Phovixay.

During the time that Manley was awaiting trial, other events were occurring in relation to crimes that Manley had committed. Investigator Kelli Schlader issued a warrant for Manley for the kidnapping of Denise Williams in Troup County in 1987, eighteen days after the kidnapping and murder of Vieng Phovixay.

The Meriwether County Grand Jury handed down a four-count indictment against Charles Manley for rape, sodomy, aggravated assault and false imprisonment in regard to the assault on Denise Williams that occurred in Meriwether County.

In cases of this magnitude, there are hundreds of hours that go into trial preparation. As is always the case, the wheels of justice turned slowly after many pretrial motions on evidence admissibility by the defense being ruled on by Judge William Smith. A trial date was set for September 5, 2007. It would finally be known if our work to find justice for Vieng would be successful and if society would be safe from the evil that dwelled among us.

Chapter 25

EVIL ON TRIAL

The trial of Charles Travis Manley for the murder of Vieng Phovixay began on September 5, 2007. The trial was contentious from the start. Ray Mayer began with his opening statement that outlined the evidence that he would present to the jury. Brian Steele answered in his opening that Charles Manley was the victim of a state conspiracy to convict an innocent man of a heinous crime he did not commit.

Steele, as we knew he would, questioned the credibility of our eyewitnesses, implying that they had been coached into identifying Manley. In all fairness, that had to be raised as a consideration, as it had been eighteen years since they had seen Manley, but we had done everything possible to protect the integrity of the identification process. Steele had even filed a motion to allow an expert witness to testify to the value of eyewitness testimony. That motion was denied by Judge Smith, as the credibility of a witness's testimony was a question to be answered by the jury. Steele went on to attack Ken Baker as being responsible for the death of Vieng Phovixay. He said the initial investigation was totally inadequate, a point on which even I would agree. From the time Vieng's remains were found in 1989, when Gary Rothwell began working the case, however, the investigation was in my opinion as thorough if not the most thorough of any I had ever been involved with. Every time the ball was dropped, it was from an administrative decision outside the hands of the investigators.

Ray laid out his case beautifully, as I knew he would. The factual witnesses all testified as to what they had seen and experienced on that fateful day

Ray Mayer, prosecuting attorney for the murder of Vieng Phovixay. *Courtesy of Ray Mayer.*

in 1987 when they last saw Vieng Phovixay. Johnny Wentz, who had the most contact that day with Manley, gave strong testimony about the conversation he had with Manley concerning the vehicle and testified that his identification was unwavering. Wentz withstood a vigorous cross-examination from Brian Steele in which he was questioned extensively about his recollection and ability to identify Manley from the lineup. Steele asked Wentz if he had been coached in any way to pick Manley from the lineup. Wentz testified emphatically that he had not been coached or pressured to make the identification.

Darlene Wentz Boynton testified as to her contact with Manley that day and affirmed that the last time she saw Vieng Phovixay she was being driven away by the man she identified as Charles Manley. On cross, Steele again attacked her recollection as to the identity of Manley and if she had been influenced in any way to pick Manley from the lineup that I had shown her. Boynton held fast to her testimony.

It was a different story when Ken Baker took the stand. He testified that he had seen the man that day with Vieng but could not with moral certainty say that he could identify the man as Manley. The car, on the other hand, was a different matter. Baker described the car in deep detail, down to the type of mag wheels; when shown a picture of Manley's El Camino, Baker said that was it without question.

Steele's cross-examination of Baker was relentless. Steele attempted to establish Baker as a neglected suspect who had a motive to kill Vieng. He questioned him extensively about the volatility of his and Vieng's relationship and about the possibility that she may have been pregnant with his child, a child he did not want. Baker was asked if during a search of his home a knife had been found, and Baker said he thought there had been a knife. There was a knife taken into evidence, and Steele may well have thought that the knife in evidence was from Baker's home. Steele made a motion for mistrial based on the fact that he was denied access to evidence that could have linked Baker to the crime. The motion was denied by Judge Smith. Through it all, Ken Baker held up well.

Steele knew if he was to win this case, he had to do it on cross-examination. Manley had put himself in Moreland on the day of Vieng's disappearance, and witnesses had put her in his company when last seen alive. The last thing he wanted to do was to put Manley up to be character assassinated by Ray on cross.

Manley's parole officer, Mike Spear, was called to testify that he had called Coweta County investigators with the tip that led to Manley being identified as a suspect.

Now, Sheriff Mike Yeager was called to testify that he had covertly taken the photograph of Manley's El Camino at his place of work and that this action had been the result of information from Mike Spear.

Ray called Gary Rothwell to testify about the extensive work he had done on the case. Gary's testimony was extensive as to the steps he had taken in the investigation. Gary was concerned that on appeal, the knife might be an issue, but he knew the only knife in evidence, and several other items recovered with it according to the evidence receipt, had been recovered from the trunk of Vieng's car found abandoned on the side of the road with a flat tire. One very important fact Gary testified to was the fact that Vieng's remains had been found approximately half a mile from a shop where Manley had once been employed in a remote part of Harris County and that he had extensive knowledge of the area where Vieng was found. After he testified, Gary went and retrieved the original GBI file, which clearly stated the knife in evidence had come from the trunk of Vieng's car. The next morning, Rothwell brought the receipt to court, where it was entered into evidence over the objection of the defense. Rothwell's quick thinking would prove invaluable upon appeal.

There were other witnesses put up relating to the events leading up to Vieng's disappearance. None of these family members and friends drew the ire of Brian Steele that I was about to.

I took the stand for the prosecution; I was asked to recall all the steps I had taken to rebuild the case. The testimony was detailed and lengthy. When Steele began his cross-examination, he knew he had to make it look as if I had a personal vendetta with Manley and that I was capable of influencing witnesses to gain a conviction. He did all he could to infuriate me, insinuating that I had prepped witnesses to sway their identifications of Manley. I realized the man had his job to do and was able to maintain my composure through his attacks on my integrity.

Then came the parade of similar circumstance witnesses; each gave a detailed account of the horrors inflicted on them at the hands of Charles

Manley. The details of brutality and deprivation were shocking. These witnesses knew Manley, and there was no doubt as to their identification of him as their attacker.

One account was especially disturbing. Gloria Tyner described the incident that took place when she was only fifteen years old. Now a brave woman in her late forties, she stared right at Manley as she wiped tears from her face and told how she was terrified as Charles Manley had held a gun to her head and raped her in 1973.

Ray Mayer opened his closing argument with a concise recount of the evidence that had been presented that called for a conviction in the case. Then came Brian Steele's close; it was a lambasting of the investigation and all those who participated in it. He alleged that Charles Manley was a victim of zealous investigators and an overeager prosecutor who would stop at nothing to obtain a conviction. He stated that witnesses had been unduly influenced and urged to perjure themselves. All this with absolutely no proof whatsoever.

Ray had the right to final closing argument, and he delivered one. In response to Steele's baseless allegations, Ray said, "Clay Bryant, thirty-year career in law enforcement, Georgia state trooper, police chief, investigator for the district attorney, investigator for the State Public Defender's Office—and he's willing to throw all that away to frame Charles Manley. Gary Rothwell, twenty-six years of distinguished service as an agent with the Georgia Bureau of Investigation—and he's willing to throw it all away to frame Charles Manley. Myself, twenty-five years in the practice of law and a prosecutor—and I'm willing to throw it all away to frame Charles Manley. That's absurd." Ray's argument was passionate.

Judge Smith charged the jury on the law that applied in the case, and they retired to deliberate. We waited for a verdict. And we waited. At the end of the day, the bailiff delivered a note from the foreman of the jury to Judge Smith saying they were unable to reach a unanimous verdict. Judge Smith gave the jury instructions and told them to reconvene the next morning and continue deliberations. This would continue for three days. On Friday, the bailiff delivered a note to Judge Smith that the jury was deadlocked at eight to four with no recent movement. I was terrified that the judge was about to declare a mistrial. Instead, the jury was brought back in and given what is known as the Adam's Charge, where the judge urges the jury to review the evidence and come to a unanimous decision, be it to convict or acquit, with instructions that they were to reconvene on Monday for another attempt to come to a verdict.

A moment of levity came the next morning when it was announced that as Shafer had been walking out of the courthouse at the end of the day, she had encountered a rattlesnake in the parking lot. The next morning, outside the presence of the jury as we awaited a verdict, Judge Smith asked Shafer, who has an excellent sense of humor, about the encounter. Shafer quickly replied that the snake had posed no threat to her, as she knew that a snake would extend professional courtesy to a person of her profession.

Monday came, and I was sure this was the last chance at deliberations before a mistrial would be declared and I would face the possibility of watching Charles Manley walk out of that courtroom once again a free man.

The jury was sent to deliberate one final time; this would certainly be the last attempt for the jury to come to a consensus. Surprisingly, after only a short while, the bailiff entered the courtroom and announced, "We have a verdict." Judge Smith instructed the bailiff to bring in the jury. The courtroom fell deathly silent as the jury filed in and was seated in the jury box. Judge Smith asked the foreman if they had a verdict. The foreman replied, "We have, your honor." The bailiff was instructed to pass the verdict to Judge Smith. Judge Smith momentarily stared at the verdict and then began to read the verdict aloud: "As to count one, malice murder, we the jury find the defendant, Charles Travis Manley, guilty."

The Phovixay family and their supporters erupted in jubilation; the Manley family cried tears of anguish. Charles Manley sank down into his chair, knowing what was about to come next.

Judge Smith ordered him to his feet and recited the sentence: "Charles Travis Manley, having been found guilty for the malice murder of Vieng Phovixay, you are hereby sentenced to life in prison in custody of the Georgia Department of Corrections." Manley was led from the courtroom.

The ordeal was over. The family and those involved in bringing the case to a successful conclusion received heartfelt congratulations from supporters. As I made the quiet drive back to my home, it was as if I could hear my dad saying, "Son, you've done well. Justice delayed was not justice denied, and that evil will no longer dwell among us."

Chapter 26

THE END OF THE ROAD

Three days after Charles Manley was convicted, his attorney Brian Steele filed a motion for a new trial in Harris County Superior Court. That motion was heard and ruled on April 21, 2008. Judge William Smith denied that motion.

Steele then followed the proper avenue of appeal and filed a motion to have the conviction of Charles Manley overturned. On January 26, 2009, the Georgia Supreme Court affirmed the conviction of Charles Manley for the malice murder of Vieng Phovixay, and his life sentence was upheld.

Charles Manley remained in prison until his death from natural causes on January 23, 2015. I have no pity or remorse for Charles Manley. My heart goes out to the victims of his heinous crimes and their families. My hope is that the work we have done helped them to find some degree of peace, for the damage that Manley caused is irreparable.

This would be my last prosecution case. Gary Rothwell, Ray Mayer and I are all retired now. Pete Skandalakis is still seeking justice as head of the Georgia Prosecuting Attorney's Council.

As I look back, my wish is that I have been able to shed some light into the darkness of our world. I think of my dad's office and a plaque that hung over his desk and its poignant words that graced that wall. When I am judged here and hereafter, I hope I have met its standard:

I Shall Pass This Way but Once.
Therefore, Any Good That I Might Do
Or Kindness I Might Show to My Fellow Man,
Let Me Do It Now.
For I Shall Not Pass This Way Again.

ABOUT THE AUTHOR

Lewis Clayton "Clay" Bryant was born and raised in Troup County, Georgia, and began his career in law enforcement in 1973 as a radio operator with the Georgia State Patrol. In 1976, at the age of twenty-one, he became the youngest trooper on the Georgia State Patrol. In 1980, he became police chief of Hogansville and stayed in that position for twelve years until resigning in 1992 and going into the private sector. He has been recognized as the most prolific cold case investigator in the United States for single-event homicides. His cases have been chronicled on *48 Hours Investigates*, *Bill Curtis's Cold Case Files*, *Discovery ID Murder Book* and the *Detective Diaries*, as well as a feature article in the *Atlanta Journal Constitution* that named him "Cold Case Clay" and described him as the cold case king. He has also appeared on numerous true crime podcasts and in articles in many local and regional newspapers.

Visit us at
www.historypress.com